Praise for *Seeking Peace*

Mairead Maguire, Nobel Peace Prize laureate
Seeking Peace inspires each of us to seek peace within our own hearts…It gives hope that we can find wholeness, happiness, and harmony, which is after all the fulfilment of God's plan for humanity.

Former Senator Bill Bradley
Seeking Peace addresses important challenges facing our society. I commend the author for seeking to assist all of us with this life-long journey.

Jonathan Kozol, author, *Amazing Grace*
Seeking Peace is a tough, transcendent envisioning of peace: neither fatuous nor sentimental, but arduous and courageous. Arnold writes in the tradition of the Berrigans, of Simone Weil and Thomas Merton. Activists of all stripes, even those who think themselves agnostics, ought not to ignore this book.

Jesse L. Jackson, The Rainbow/PUSH Coalition
A splendid book drawing on the rich experiences of the author and on relevant observations by legendary activists and writers…A valuable contribution to contemporary thought, and a guide for action as the struggle continues.

Brother David Steindl-Rast, Mount Saviour Monastery
Seeking Peace is a book for people who realize that we are fish out of water. Arnold speaks out of a living tradition of radical response to the challenge of one whose very name is Peace. There is living water here for gasping fish.

Muhammed Gemea'ah, The Islamic Cultural Center of N.Y.
An excellent work… *Seeking Peace* is the very essence of what we are all about.

Tony Campolo, Eastern College
Everybody talks about peace, even as they prepare for war. This is a book that talks about peace in a way that prepares us to make it happen.

John C. Dwyer, St. Bernard's Institute
Seeking Peace is profoundly and universally human. None of the problems of contemporary life are missing, but there is no finger-waving or pietistic jargon...There is a lifetime's material for meditation, and an abundance of life in it. This book deserves to become a classic.

Thomas Howard, St. John's Seminary
Seeking Peace is a gem. The candor, simplicity, and humanity of the whole text, and especially of the anecdotes, should recommend it to an exceedingly wide reading public.

Elizabeth McAlister, Jonah House
An incisive gospel book on a critical issue. May it help Christians regain their lost heritage of justice and peace.

Bernard Häring, author, *Virtues of an Authentic Life*
A thoughtful and attractive vision of a truly dedicated Christian life...and a convincing testimony to a truly ecumenical spirit. Readers will be grateful for the depth and insights of this outstanding author.

Philip Berrigan, Plowshares
Seeking Peace has a lucidity and power completely comprehensible to any person of good will. Peace is the central characteristic of the Gospel, and it is too often avoided or ignored.

Thomas Green, author, *When the Well Runs Dry*
Seeking Peace is solidly rooted in the Christian – and even Jewish and Buddhist – tradition. As Arnold reminds us, Jesus' peace has nothing to do with passivity, nor is it for the spineless or self-absorbed. It demands deeds of love.

Rev. William N. Grosch, M.D., Albany Medical College
Seeking Peace is a delight to read. It is measured and well balanced, and as in Arnold's previous books, the rich human stories make for compelling reading...I will enthusiastically recommend this book to my family, friends, and colleagues. It is another support for me and my work.

Seeking Peace

Seeking Peace

Notes and Conversations Along the Way

Johann Christoph Arnold

Foreword by Madeleine L'Engle

Preface by Thich Nhat Hanh

Plough Publishing House

Published by Plough Publishing House
Rifton, New York
Robertsbridge, England
Elsmore, Australia
www.plough.com

© 2013 by Plough Publishing House
Introduction © 2000 by Plough Publishing House
All Rights Reserved.

ISBN: 978-0-87486-963-7

Cover photograph © Paul Clancy.
Foreword by Madeleine L'Engle © 1998 by Crosswicks, Ltd.
Preface © 1998 by Thich Nhat Hanh

Excerpt from *Murder in the Cathedral* by T. S. Eliot. Copyright 1935 by Harcourt,
Inc. and renewed 1963 by T. S. Eliot. Reprinted by permission of Houghton Mifflin
Harcourt Publishing Company. All rights reserved.

The material from Dale Aukerman on pages 99–101 appeared in revised form in
The Brethren Messenger, April 1998, and is used with permission of the author.

First Edition (hardcover) © 1998, ISBN 978-0-87486-958-7
Second Edition (softcover) © 1999, ISBN 0-87486-963-3
20 19 18 17 16 15 14   3 4 5 6 7 8 9 10 11 12

A catalog record for this book is available from the British Library.

Library of Congress Cataloging-in-Publication Data

Arnold, Johann Christoph, 1940-
  Seeking peace : notes and conversations along the way / Johann Christoph Arnold ;
  foreword by Madeleine L'Engle ; preface by Thich Nhat Hanh.
    p. cm.
  Includes index.
  ISBN 978-0-87486-963-7 (pbk.)
  1. Peace of mind--Religious aspects. 2. Peace--Religious aspects. I. Title.
  BL627.55A76 2013
  201'.7273--dc23

                    2012042052

Printed in the USA

NOW THINK FOR A MOMENT about the meaning of this word "peace." Does it seem strange to you that the angels should have announced Peace, when ceaselessly the world has been stricken with War and the fear of War? Does it seem to you that the angelic voices were mistaken, and that the promise was a disappointment and a cheat?

Reflect now, how Our Lord Himself spoke of Peace. He said to His disciples, "Peace I leave with you, my peace I give unto you." Did He mean peace as we think of it: the kingdom of England at peace with its neighbors, the barons at peace with the King, the householder counting over his peaceful gains, the swept hearth, his best wine for a friend at the table, his wife singing to the children? Those men, His disciples, knew no such things: they went forth to journey afar, to suffer by land and sea, to know torture, imprisonment, disappointment, to suffer death by martyrdom. What then did He mean? If you ask that, remember then that He said also, "Not as the world gives, give I unto you." So then, He gave to His disciples peace, but not peace as the world gives.

T. S. Eliot
Murder in the Cathedral

Acknowledgments

Dozens of people helped bring this book into print, but I would especially like to thank my editor, Chris Zimmerman; my secretaries, Emmy Maria Blough, Hanna Rimes, and Ellen Keiderling; and the entire staff of the Plough Publishing House.

I would also like to thank those who allowed me to use anecdotes and letters, and those who supported me in other ways as I worked on this book: Imam Muhammed Salem Agwa, Dale Aukerman, Daniel Berrigan, Philip Berrigan, Rabbi Kenneth L. Cohen, Tom Cornell, Fr. Benedict Groeschel, Thich Nhat Hanh, Molly Kelly, Frances Kieffer, Sr. Ann LaForest, Madeleine L'Engle, Rev. William Marvin, Elizabeth McAlister, Bill Pelke, and Bishop Samuel Ruíz García – not to mention numerous fellow members of my community.

Above all I thank my wife, Verena. Without her encouragement and support, this book could not have been written.

Contents

Foreword
by Madeleine L'Engle

Shalom. Peace. A peace that is not passive, but active. A peace that is not just the cessation of violence, but is through and beyond violence. Real peace.

In an era that has been notable for its lack of peace, it is good to have Johann Christoph Arnold's fine book, *Seeking Peace*. He quotes his grandfather's definition of peace: "the inner peace of the soul with God; the fulfillment of nonviolence, through peaceful relationships with others; and the establishment of a just and peaceful social order." As I listen to the news each morning, we seem to be slipping further and further away from this threefold peace. We need this book which guides us to Shalom.

A decade or so ago one evening during Lent, at Manhattan's Cathedral Church of St. John the Divine, I listened to the Reverend Canon Edward West talk about the peace we seek, and use the rather unexpected metaphor of a subway.

Most of us in the audience that night rode the subway, to the Cathedral, to and from work. He pointed out to us that if we looked at the people riding in the same car with us, most of them would look as though nobody loved them. And that, alas, was largely true. Then he told us that if we would concentrate inconspicuously on one person, affirming silently that this person was a beloved child of God, and, no matter what the circumstances, could lie in God's peace, we might see a difference. Peace is not always something you "do;" it is a gift you can give.

The next time I rode the subway I glanced at a woman in the corner, hunched over, hands clenched, an expression of resigned endurance on her face. So, without looking at her,

I began to try to send God's loving peace to her. I didn't move. I didn't stare at her. I simply followed Canon West's suggestion, and to my wonder she began to relax. Her hands unclenched; her body relaxed; the lines of anxiety left her face. It was a moment for me of great gratitude, and a peace that spread out and filled me too.

It is something I try to remember as I ride a subway or bus, or walk down the crowded streets, or stand in slow-moving lines at the supermarket. If God's peace is in our hearts, we carry it with us, and it can be given to those around us, not by our own will or virtue, but by the Holy Spirit working through us. We cannot give what we do not have, but if the spirit blows through the dark clouds, and enters our hearts, we can be used as vehicles of peace, and our own peace will be thereby deepened. The more peace we give away, the more we have.

In *Seeking Peace,* Arnold tells of many such incidents, illustrating as well as explaining the kind of peace he calls us to seek. This is an important as well as a beautiful book, and a much needed one to help us take God's peace with us into the future.

Goshen, Connecticut
Summer 1998

Preface
by Thich Nhat Hanh

In the Sermon on the Mount, Jesus says, "Blessed are the peacemakers, for they shall be called the children of God." To work for peace, you must have a peaceful heart. When you do, you are a child of God. But many who work for peace are not at peace. They still have anger and frustration, and their work is not really peaceful. We cannot say that they are touching the kingdom of God. To preserve peace, our hearts must be at peace with the world, with our brothers and our sisters. This truth is at the heart of Johann Christoph Arnold's welcome new book, *Seeking Peace*.

We often think of peace as the absence of war; that if the powerful countries would reduce their arsenals, we could have peace. But if we look deeply into the weapons, we see our own minds—our prejudices, fears, and ignorance. Even if we transported all the bombs to the moon, the roots of war and the reasons for bombs would still be here, in our hearts and minds, and sooner or later we would make new bombs.

Jesus said, "It is written, 'Thou shalt not kill; and whosoever shall kill shall be in danger of judgment.' But I say unto you, that whosoever is angry with his brother without cause shall be in danger of the judgment...Whosoever shall say, 'Thou fool,' shall be in danger of hell fire." So working for peace must mean more than getting rid of weapons. It must start with uprooting war from ourselves and from the hearts of all men and women.

How can we end the cycle of violence? Arnold tells us that before we can make peace with others and with the world, we must make peace with ourselves. How true this is! If we are at war with our parents, our family, our society, or our church, there is probably a war going on inside us also. Therefore the most basic work for peace is to return to ourselves and create harmony among the elements within us – our feelings, our perceptions, our mental states.

As you read this book, seek to recognize the conflicting elements within you and their underlying causes. Seek to become more aware of what causes anger and separation, and what overcomes them. Root out the violence in your life, and learn to live compassionately and mindfully. Seek peace. When you have peace within, real peace with others will be possible.

Village des Pruniers, France
Spring 1998

Introduction

It has been years since the first edition of this book appeared, and the rising tide of violence I wrote about then has since become a wave that threatens to engulf everything in its path. Not a day goes by, it seems, without murder or mayhem of some sort. Violence is everywhere, whereas peace is almost nowhere to be found. Rather than discourage us, though, this ought to jolt us out of our complacency and spur us to action.

Peace activist Dorothy Day, whom I first met some forty years ago, once wrote, "No one has a right to sit down and feel hopeless. There is too much work to do." Writing this book has put me in touch with countless readers who share her determination. It has resulted in letters from the Vatican and the White House, and hundreds from more ordinary addresses as well. It even brought a response from a convicted murderer, in the bowels of death row in Texas, who wrote:

> Have you ever seen the movie *The Mission?* In it a slaver who has killed his brother in a duel does penance by hauling his armor up the rocky side of a waterfall over and over, until he is satisfied that it is enough. In the end he finds his peace. I'm still seeking mine.
>
> I'm not sure why I'm writing to you…it's so hard to find someone to write to who is capable of understanding my struggle…But I just finished reading *Seeking Peace,* and I want you to know that this has been one of the most meaningful books I've ever read. It really put some fire in these tired bones.

Another letter that touched me was this one, from a woman in Kentucky:

> Reading *Seeking Peace* has become a spiritual practice for me. I feel like the men and women quoted in it are talking to me personally….

I grieve for the hatred and violence in the world, and for the poverty around me, which is often a poverty of spirit as much as a lack of material goods. What can any of us really do in the face of the needs of this world? I think we must pray; we must live as consciously as we can, and take steps to overcome our own weaknesses. We must also give to others whenever we have the opportunity, and not hoard our wealth, whatever form it is in. And all the while we must, as Mother Teresa said, be faithful in the small things.

Most gratifying of all, I have heard from dozens of younger readers whose lives have been touched by the stories in this book. In Littleton, Colorado, for example, a youth group had been using *Seeking Peace* for a weekly book discussion that continued for several months. When I spoke at their church some time later, several of the participants told me how deeply it had affected them. Then, in the last week of April 1999, as news of the Littleton high school massacre was making headlines across the country, I learned that one of the victims, Cassie Bernall, had been part of this youth group, and that she was planning to attend a final discussion of the book on the day she was killed. Immediately my mind leapt to a line from the Gospel of John—a verse that for me captures one of the most vital truths there is about finding peace: "Unless the seed dies and is buried, it will only remain a seed. But when it dies, it produces many seeds." Already, stories of Cassie's faith (she affirmed her belief in God at gunpoint) were spreading beyond her hometown, and she has since become a symbol of conviction for millions of people around the world.

Several of those who shared their stories with me for this book have now passed on. In each case, it has struck me that because they had truly found peace, nothing could take it away—neither pain, uncertainty, nor fear of the future. Peace was the greatest gift they possessed.

Dale Aukerman went on planting trees at his Maryland farm until cancer confined him to his bed, and after that he spent his time writing and dictating letters. George Burleson, who also succumbed to cancer, visited prison inmates for as long as he could and insisted, during the final stages of his illness, on being driven to a rally against capital punishment. Both men must have feared death on some level, but because they had found peace, they were able to lay aside their self-concern and reach out to others until the end. Both went peacefully, and with confidence.

The words of another person in this book, Freda Dyroff, who has died since its initial publication, gained special significance in light of the Littleton massacre. A few weeks after the shooting I was speaking in Denver and was shown Cassie Bernall's personal copy of *Seeking Peace*. Among other passages that she had highlighted was this one from Freda:

> Seek until you find, and don't give up. Pray, too, even if you think you don't believe, because God hears even the "unbeliever" as she groans. God will help you through. Don't give up, and above all, avoid the temptations that distract you from what you know you really long for. If you do fall, pick yourself up again and get back on track.

Though hardly dramatic, this coincidence reminds me that more often than not, peace grows quietly and invisibly, like a seed in the heart. Freda is now gone, and Cassie, too, but—like every kernel that disintegrates and dies—the seeds of their peace have sent up new shoots. And as we look to the future, rather than bemoaning the sorry state of our world, we can water and nourish those seeds.

Johann Christoph Arnold
Rifton, New York

Seeking Peace

"Hope is the thing left to us in a bad time."
Irish Proverb

Seeking Peace

We live in an unpeaceful world, and despite constant talk about peace, there is very little. So little, in fact, that when I told a close friend about this book, he suggested it was not only naïve to write on the topic, but even somewhat perverse.

No one will deny that violence affects public life everywhere around our globe, from current hot spots overseas to the streets of our own decaying cities. In personal life too, even in the most "peaceful" suburbs, unpeace is often the order of the day – in domestic violence, in unhealthy addictions, and in the destructive tensions that divide businesses, schools, and churches.

Violence hides behind the most respectable façades of our supposedly enlightened society. It is there in the turbines of greed, deceit, and injustice that drive our greatest financial and cultural institutions. It is there in the unfaithfulness that can erode even the best "Christian" marriages. It is there in the hypocrisy that deadens spiritual life and robs the most devout expressions of religion of their credibility.

The need for peace cries to heaven. It is one of the deepest longings of the heart. Call it what you will: harmony, serenity, wholeness, soundness of mind – the yearning for it exists somewhere in every human being. No one likes problems, headaches, heartaches. Everyone wants peace – freedom from anxiety and doubt, violence and division. Everyone wants stability and security.

Some people and organizations (the International Fellowship of Reconciliation comes to mind) focus on striving for global peace. Their goal is the attainment of political cooperation on an international scale. Others (like Green-peace) seek to promote harmony between human beings and other living things, and a consciousness of our inter-relatedness with the environment.

Others look for peace by modifying their lifestyles: by changing careers, moving from the city to the suburbs (or from the suburbs to the country), cutting back, simplifying, or otherwise improving their quality of life. Then there is the young man who recently returned home to my com-munity from abroad: after a "wild ride" of fast money and promiscuous relationships, he yearns to be able "to wake up in the morning and be at peace with myself and with God." Still others seem to be at ease with the lives they lead; happy and fulfilled, they claim they are not searching for anything. Yet I suspect that below the surface, even these people do not possess perfect peace.

While working on this book I came across an ad with a picture of a woman on a dock. Curled up in a lawn chair, she is gazing out over a lake toward a brilliant sunset. The ad reads: "A dream job. Beautiful kids. The best marriage. And a gnawing feeling of absolute emptiness." How many millions share her unspoken fear?

At a certain level, we are all in search of life as the Creator intended it: a life where harmony, joy, justice, and peace rule. Each of us has dreamed of the life where sorrow and pain do not exist, of the lost Eden for which (the Bible says) all creation groans.

The longing for such a time and place is as ancient as it is universal. Thousands of years ago, the Hebrew prophet Isaiah dreamed of a peaceable kingdom where the lion would dwell with the lamb. And down through the centu-ries, no matter how dark the horizon or bloody the battle-field, men and women have found hope in his vision.

When anti-war activist Philip Berrigan was tried and sentenced for committing civil disobedience at a naval shipyard in Maine in 1997, many people dismissed his actions. Phil admitted that by most standards they "constituted a theater of the absurd." But he added that he would rather spend the rest of his life in prison for his convictions, than die "on some beach." How many of us can say the same? Although in his seventies, Phil continued his tireless campaign against the nuclear weapons industry with such vigor that one all but forgot his age.

My own community, the Bruderhof, has often been similarly accused of being out of touch with reality. Yes, we have abandoned the accepted path to middle-class happiness – the route of private homes and property, careers, bank accounts, mutual funds, and comfortable retirement – in order to try to live together in the manner of the first Christians. We struggle to live a life of sacrifice and discipline and mutual service. It is not a life of peace as the world gives.

What is peace, and what is reality? What are we living for, and what do we want to pass on to our children and grandchildren? Even if we are happy, what will we have left after the marriage and the kids, after the car and the job? Must our legacy really be the "reality" of a world bristling with weapons, a world of class hatreds and family grievances, a world of lovelessness and backbiting, selfish ambition and spite? Or is there a greater reality, where all these are overcome by the power of the Prince of Peace?

In the following pages I have tried to resist formulating neat theses or presenting loophole-proof arguments. Spiritual "how-to" guides can be found in any bookstore, though in my experience life is never so tidy. Often it is very messy. In any case, each reader will be at a different place in his or her search. I have also tried to avoid dwelling on the roots of unpeace. One could focus a whole book on that subject, but it would be too depressing to wade through. My aim, very simply, is to offer you stepping stones along the way – and enough hope to keep you seeking peace.

II

Meanings

"Only when you have made peace
within yourself will you be able
to make peace in the world."
Rabbi Simcha Bunim

Meanings

From greeting cards to bookmarks, from billboards to embroidered dish towels, our culture is awash in the language of peace. Phrases such as "peace and good will" appear so widely that they have been reduced to slogans and clichés. In correspondence, many of us close personal letters with "Peace." On another level, governments and the mass media speak of heavily armed "peace-keeping" battalions stationed in war-torn regions around the world. In churches, priests and ministers close their services with "Go in peace," and though the words are intended as a blessing, they often seem to be little more than a dismissal until the following Sunday.

Muhammad Salem Agwa, a leading *Imam* (Islamic teacher) in New York, notes that observant Muslims acknowledge each other when they meet with the words *Salaam alaikum*. Yet he says that among them, too, the greeting of peace has all too often become a habit, passed on with little regard for the mutual responsibilities it implies:

> I use *Salaam alaikum* as a daily greeting, but it does not just mean "Good morning" or "Good afternoon." It means more: "The peace and blessings of God be upon you." When I say this, I feel that you are at peace with me, and I with you. I am extending a helping hand to you. I am coming to you to give you peace. And in the meantime, until we meet again, it means that I pray to God to bless you and have mercy upon you, and to strengthen my relationship to you as a brother.

How different the world would be if we were really at peace with everyone we greet during the course of the day, if our words were more than politeness and came from our hearts! In reality, as atheists never tire of pointing out, few conflicts have caused so much bloodshed in the course of human history as our ceaseless bickering over religious differences. No wonder the old prophets sighed, "They lead my people astray saying, 'Peace, peace,' when there is no peace."

Peace as the Absence of War

To many people, peace means national security, stability, law and order. It is associated with education, culture, and civic duty, prosperity and health, comfort and quiet. It is the good life. But can a peace based on these things be shared by all? If the good life means limitless choices and excessive consumption for a privileged few, it follows that it must mean hard labor and grinding poverty for millions of others. Can this be peace?

Writing on the eve of World War ii, my grandfather, Eberhard Arnold, wrote:

> Does pacifism suffice? I don't think it is enough.
>
> When over a thousand people have been killed unjustly, without trial, under Hitler's new government, isn't that already war?
>
> When hundreds of thousands of people in concentration camps are robbed of their freedom and stripped of all human dignity, isn't that war?
>
> When in Asia millions of people starve to death while in North America and elsewhere millions of tons of wheat are stockpiled, isn't that war?
>
> When thousands of women prostitute their bodies and ruin their lives for the sake of money; when millions of babies are aborted each year, isn't that war?
>
> When people are forced to work like slaves because they can hardly provide the milk and bread for their children, isn't that war?
>
> When the wealthy live in villas surrounded by parks, while in other districts some families have only one room to share, isn't that war?
>
> When one person builds up a huge bank account while another earns scarcely enough for basic necessities, isn't that war?

When reckless drivers cause thousands of traffic deaths every year, isn't that war?

I cannot represent a pacifism that maintains there will be no more war. This claim is not valid; there is war right up to the present day...I cannot agree with a pacifism whose representatives hold onto the root causes of war: property and capitalism. I have no faith in the pacifism of businessmen who beat down their competitors, or husbands who cannot even live in peace and love with their own wives...

I would rather not use the word "pacifism" at all. But I am an advocate of peace. Jesus said, "Blessed are the peacemakers!" If I really want peace, I must represent it in all areas of life.

In political terms, peace may take the form of trade agreements, compromises, and peace treaties. Such treaties are usually little more than fragile balances of power negotiated in tense settings, and often they plant seeds of new conflicts worse than the ones they were designed to resolve. There are many examples, from the Treaty of Versailles, which ended World War I but stoked the nationalism that started World War II, to the Yalta Conference, which ended World War II but fueled tensions that led to the Cold War. Ceasefires provide no guarantee of an end to hatred.

Everyone agrees that peace is the answer to war, but what kind of peace? Rabbi Kenneth L. Cohen writes:

Darkness is the absence of light, but peace is not just the cessation of hostilities. Treaties may be signed, ambassadors exchanged, and armies sent home, yet there still may not be peace. Peace is metaphysical and cosmic in its implications. It is more than the absence of war. Peace, in fact, is not the absence of anything, but rather the ultimate affirmation of what can be.

Peace in the Bible

One way to examine the deeper meanings of peace is to see what the Bible says about it. In the Old Testament there is perhaps no concept richer than the Hebrew word for peace: *shalom*. Shalom is difficult to translate because of the depth and breadth of its connotations. It possesses no single meaning, though one might translate it as completeness, soundness, or wholeness. It extends far beyond "peace" as we commonly think of it in the English language.

Shalom means the end of war and conflict, but it also means friendship, contentment, security, and health; prosperity, abundance, tranquility, harmony with nature, and even salvation. And it means these things for everyone, not only a select few. Shalom is ultimately a blessing, a gift from God. It is not a human endeavor. It applies to the state of the individual, but also to relationships – among people and nations, and between God and man. Beyond this, shalom is intimately tied to justice, because it is the enjoyment or celebration of human relationships which have been made right.

In his book *He Is Our Peace*, Howard Goeringer illustrates an even more radical meaning of shalom: love of one's enemies.

> In 600 BC the Babylonian army invaded Judea and took hostages from Jerusalem into exile. It was in such difficult circumstances that Jeremiah wrote these remarkable words to refugees in hated Babylon: "Seek the shalom of the city where I have sent you into exile, and pray to the Lord on its behalf, for in its shalom you will find your shalom." The refugees were forced to live as exiles while they watched their Jewish culture collapse. Despising their captors, yearning to return to their homeland, and resenting God's failure to save

them, they couldn't believe what Jeremiah was saying. This crazy man of God was telling them to love their captors, to do good to their enemies, to ask the Lord to bless their persecutors with shalom.

As we might expect, Jeremiah's letter was not popular, not a bestseller. The suffering hostages could not see how their well-being and the well-being of their captors were inseparably bound together. To think of serving their captors in a spirit of kindness, nursing their sick, teaching their children Jewish games, working an extra hour for them! – this was utter foolishness.

Goeringer is right: often the peace of God appears utterly irrational, not only in the eyes of the worldly-wise, but in the eyes of the most religious people.

Peace is a central theme in the New Testament too, where the word *eirene* is used most frequently. In its biblical context, *eirene* extends far beyond its classical Greek meaning, "rest," and includes many of the various connotations of shalom. In the New Testament, Jesus the Messiah is the bearer, sign, and instrument of God's peace. In fact, Paul says Christ is our peace. In him all things are reconciled. That is why his message is called the gospel of peace. It is the good news of God's coming reign, where all is made right.

Peace as a Social Cause

The world is full of activists fighting for worthy causes: there are advocates for the environment and for the homeless, anti-war activists and promoters of social justice, fighters on behalf of battered women and oppressed minorities, and on and on. In the sixties many of us in the religious community marched with Martin Luther King. In the nineties, many took up the fight for the abolition of the death penalty. This cause is, in a broader sense, a struggle against the injustices in the American judicial system. The horrors I have come across, both locally and internationally, make it clear that the politics of law and order have more to do with violence and fear than with peace.

Some of the men and women I have come to know in this work are among the most dedicated people I have ever met, and I would not belittle their achievements for a minute. Yet the fragmentation that marks the lives of others, and the divisiveness that often results in their fighting one another, is painfully apparent too.

Looking back on the sixties, a time when so-called peaceniks abounded, several thoughts come to mind. The longing of Beatles fans who chanted "Give peace a chance" over and over cannot be discounted; I feel it was genuinely spiritual. Unlike the overwhelming majority of today's young men and women, many youth in the sixties and seventies attempted to translate their hopes and dreams into deeds. They led marches and held events, formed communes and committed acts of civil disobedience; they organized sit-ins, protests, and community service projects. No one could accuse them of being apathetic. Yet it is hard to forget the anger that twisted the faces of some who shouted loudest for peace in those years, and the anarchy and cynicism that later swallowed the whole era.

What happens when idealism runs out, when the rally is finished, when the Summer of Love is over? What happens when peaceful communes and loving relationships fall apart? Does peace become just another cultural commodity, a symbol to be ironed on T-shirts or printed on bumper stickers? In *The Long Loneliness*, Dorothy Day, the legendary radical who founded the Catholic Worker, comments that youth's longing for a better world sometimes has as much to do with nihilism and selfishness as with anything else. Young people idealize change, she says, but they are rarely ready to start with themselves. To quote Rabbi Cohen again:

> An individual can march for peace or vote for peace and can have, perhaps, some small influence on global concerns. But the same small individual is a giant in the eyes of a child at home. If peace is to be built, it must start with the individual. It is built brick by brick.

Peace in Personal Life

Sylvia Beels came to our community from London as a young woman, just before the outbreak of the Second World War. She told me that a prevalent attitude in the peace movement of her youth – an opposition to killing, but not to social injustice – dissatisfied her and made her want to seek something more:

> A war film I saw when I was nine horrified me, and from then on I knew I could never see war as anything good, however good the cause might be.
>
> After I married, my husband Raymond and I joined the Left Book Club and read all their books. We met regularly with a group of friends discussing the ideas in these books. We searched and searched to find a way through the labyrinth of human ideas – war, peace, politics, conventional morals versus free love, etc. – but came no nearer to finding a peaceful or just society.

Later, during the long, difficult birth of her first child, Sylvia realized that her personal life was marked by the very same troubles she was fighting in society. Despite a promising career in music, her marriage was in shambles and her mind in turmoil. Then and there she decided that before she could contribute anything to world peace, she needed to find peace within herself and with others. (Sylvia's husband died of heart disease shortly after this, but they were able to reconcile at his deathbed.)

Maureen Burn, another community member, came to the same conclusion after years of anti-war activism, first in Edinburgh and then in Birmingham, where money, social connections, and a vibrant personality made her a well-known and effective pacifist:

I was always an idealist and a rebel. The First World War worried me, though I was but a child. We were told that the German Kaiser had caused the war, and when I was ten I wrote to him asking him please to stop the war. I was always against war.

My husband, Matthew, a prominent public-health officer, was also a pacifist. After experiencing the trenches of World War I, he had become an ardent anti-militarist and champion of social justice. Our common interest in the Russian Revolution of 1918, the works of Tolstoy, and the crusades of Gandhi had created a bond between us and led to marriage.

Many young people were going to Moscow in those years, and because we were attracted to the communist ideal, "from each according to his strength, to each according to his need," I suggested that we move to Russia, too, with our little boys…Only when Matthew said, "A bomb thrown by a communist is no better than a bomb thrown by a capitalist" did I change my mind.

Matthew always disappeared on Armistice Day. I don't know where he went. He thought it an insult to the dead to have a big military parade at the Cenotaph, where the unknown soldier was buried; and he never wore his medals. After the war Matthew's mother told me that he had once declared he would never again do a thing for a society so rotten that even the clergy preached killing to the young…

In the Second World War, during the bombing of Britain, many English cities began to evacuate children, and the Burns had to find a place to take their four sons, the youngest not yet one year old. Matthew's job required that he stay in the city, and Maureen had no idea where to go. Just in those same days Maureen discovered she was pregnant with a fifth child. Under these uncertain circumstances, she and Matthew decided for an abortion.

When I returned home afterward, my husband suggested I go to my sister Kathleen for a few days' rest. Kathleen lived at an intentional community. I wrote asking if I could come for a short time, and she answered yes.

I had no idea what a shock awaited me there. I was reading some of their literature, I can't remember the title of the book. Whatever it was, it plainly stated that abortion was murder: to kill new life in the womb was no more justifiable in the eyes of God than the killing that takes place in war. Up till then I had been a rationalist and didn't see anything terrible about abortion. Now, however, I was thrown into great turmoil and felt the horror of my action for the first time.

I do not cry easily, but at that point I could do nothing but weep and weep. I deeply regretted what I had done, and longed that it could be undone. I was only a visitor to the community, but my sister took me to one of the ministers, and I told him all. He invited me to a members' meeting, where a prayer was said for me. Immediately I knew I was forgiven. It was a miracle, a gift; I was full of joy and peace, and able to make a new start in life.

Nothing is so vital – or painful – as recognizing the unpeace in our own lives and hearts. For some of us it may be hatred or resentment; with others, deceit, dividedness, or confusion; still others, mere emptiness or depression. In the deepest sense it is all violence and must therefore be faced and overcome. Thomas Merton writes:

> There is a very pervasive form of contemporary violence to which the idealist fighting for peace by nonviolent methods most easily succumbs: activism and overwork. The rush and pressure of modern life are a form, perhaps the most common form, of its innate violence. To allow oneself to be carried away by a multitude of conflicting concerns, to surrender to too many demands, to commit oneself to too many projects, to want to help everyone in everything is to succumb

to violence. More than that, it is cooperation in violence. The frenzy of the activist neutralizes his work for peace. It destroys the fruitfulness of his own work, because it kills the root of inner wisdom which makes work fruitful.

Many people feel called to take up the cause of peace, but most of them turn back once they realize that they cannot bring it to others unless they experience it themselves. Unable to find harmony in their own lives, they soon come to the end of their rope.

In the most tragic instances, a person may suffer such disillusionment that he takes his own life. Folk singer Phil Ochs, a well-known peace activist in the sixties, comes to mind; so does Mitch Snyder, founder of the Center for Creative Nonviolence and a respected advocate for the homeless in Washington, D.C.

The Peace of God

True peace is not merely a lofty cause that can be taken up and pursued with good intentions. Nor is it something to be simply had or bought. Peace demands struggle. It is found by taking up the fundamental battles of life: life versus death, good versus evil, truth versus falsehood. Yes, it is a gift, but it is also the result of the most intense striving. In fact, several verses in the Psalms imply that it is in the process of striving for peace that peace is found. Such peace is a consequence of confronting and overcoming conflict, not avoiding it. And rooted as it is in righteousness, genuine peace – the peace of God – disrupts false relationships, disturbs wrongful systems, and debunks the lies that promise a false peace. It uproots the seeds of unpeace.

God's peace does not automatically include inner tranquility, the absence of conflict, or other, worldly estimations of peace. As we can see from the life of Christ, it was precisely by his rejection of the world and its peace that his perfect peace was established. And this peace was rooted in his acceptance of the most harrowing self-sacrifice imaginable: death on a cross.

Many of us who call ourselves Christians today have forgotten this, if not willfully blinded ourselves to it. We want peace, but we want it on our own terms. We want an easy peace. Yet peace cannot come quickly or easily if it is to have any genuine staying power. It cannot merely mean psychological well-being or equilibrium, a pleasant feeling that is here today and gone tomorrow. The peace of God is more than a state of consciousness. Dorothy Sayers writes:

> I believe it to be a great mistake to present Christianity as something charming and popular with no offense in it... We cannot blink at the fact that gentle Jesus meek and mild

was so stiff in his opinions and so inflammatory in his language that he was thrown out of church, stoned, hunted from place to place, and finally gibbeted as a firebrand and a public danger. Whatever his peace was, it was not the peace of an amiable indifference.

Here I should point out that despite my own faith in Christ, and despite the vocabulary of this book (which some may find "churchy") I do not believe that one must necessarily be a Christian to find the peace of Jesus. True, we cannot ignore Jesus' statements: "He who does not gather with me, scatters" and "He who is not for me is against me." Yet what does it mean to be "for" Jesus? Doesn't he make it clear that it is not religious words or other expressions of piety that matter? He looks for deeds of compassion and mercy – for love. And he says that even giving a cup of water to a thirsty person will be rewarded "in the kingdom of heaven."

Jesus is a person, not a concept or an article of theology, and his truth embraces far more than our limited minds can comprehend. In any case, millions of Buddhists, Muslims, Jews – and agnostics and atheists – practice the love Jesus commands us to live out with more conviction than many so-called Christians. And it is hardly our place to say whether or not they possess his peace.

The Peace that Passes Understanding

Some readers might find it fruitful if I went on here to examine various understandings of peace, and to discuss whether it is a way or a state of being. Others might wish to know just what I mean when I say people are seeking peace. Are they looking for closeness with others, or hungering to be themselves? Are they yearning for trust and love, for something more to look forward to than retirement? Something else entirely? What is peace, in a nutshell? A thought from one of my grandfather's books has been helpful to me. He writes about a threefold peace: the inner peace of the soul with God; the fulfillment of non-violence through peaceful relationships with others; and the establishment of a just and peaceful social order.

In the end, though, the best definition does not matter, for it may not help us find peace. To grasp the meaning of peace we must experience it as a practical reality, not only as something in the head, or even in the heart, but in our day-to-day lives.

Sadhu Sundar Singh, a Christian Indian mystic who lived at the turn of the 20th century, writes:

> The secret and reality of a blissful life in God cannot be understood without receiving, living, and experiencing it. If we try to understand it only with the intellect, we will find our efforts useless.
>
> A scientist had a bird in his hand. He saw that it had life and, wanting to find out in what part of the bird's body its life lay, he began dissecting the bird. The result was that the very life he was in search of disappeared. Those who try to understand the mysteries of the inner life intellectually will

meet with similar failure. The life they are looking for will vanish in the analysis.

As water is restless until it has reached its level, so the soul has no peace until it rests in God.

Paradoxes

"I am a soldier of Christ; I cannot fight."

St. Martin of Tours

Paradoxes

We have already seen that though the yearning for peace is a deep, universal hunger, it is hard to define. The same is true of most things of the spirit. Elias Chacour, a Palestinian priest and a good friend of mine, comments on this in his book *Blood Brothers*. Speaking of the great Eastern religions, he notes that their thinkers (in contrast to many in our western culture) are comfortable with paradoxes and willing to accept them and live with them rather than discard them.

Anyone who has read the Gospels knows how Jesus relied on paradoxes and parables to illustrate profound truths. To the rational mind a paradox may seem contradictory, yet just because of this, it forces us to look at the truth in it with new eyes. In this sense I have written the following sections, each of which provides a springboard toward a deeper understanding of peace.

Not Peace, but a Sword

Don't imagine that I came to bring peace to the earth! No, rather, a sword. I have come to set a man against his father, and a daughter against her mother, and a daughter-in-law against her mother-in-law — a man's worst enemies will be found right in his own home! If you love your father and mother more than you love me, you are not worthy of being mine; or if you love your son or daughter more than me, you are not worthy of being mine.

Jesus of Nazareth

When Matthew recorded these words of Jesus in the tenth chapter of his Gospel, he gave generations of Christians a favorite argument with which to defend the use of force in dealing with other human beings. But what did Jesus really mean? Certainly he could not have meant to justify or promote armed violence. Even if he drove the moneychangers from the temple with a whip, he later chided Peter for cutting off a soldier's ear and said, "He who takes up the sword shall perish by the sword." And his deeds, right up to his last breath on the cross, are mirrored in his words, "Do unto others as you would have others do to you."

To me it is clear that the sword Jesus was referring to has nothing to do with any weapon of human warfare. In the letters of the apostle Paul we read of the sword of the Spirit as compared to the sword of government authority, which is variously called the temporal sword or the sword of God's wrath. Paul concedes that God withdrew the Holy Spirit from the world because men and women would not obey him; instead, he gave them the "sword" of earthly governments, whose stability and authority is rooted in their military power. But the church must make no use of physical weapons. It must remain loyal to one power: Christ. His true followers wield only the sword of the Spirit.

Elsewhere in the Bible the sword is used as a symbol of truth. Like the physical weapon it represents, this sword cuts through everything that binds us to sin. It cleans and exposes (the writer of the Letter to the Hebrews says it "divides joints and marrow"), yet its purpose is not destruction or death. To quote British poet Philip Britts, peace is "the weaponry of love and redemption...not carnal weaponry, but the weaponry of the will to Truth." Its war is not the striving of men against each other, but of "the creator against the destroyer; the war of the will to life against the will to death; the war of love against hate, of unity against separation."

In the gospel we read, "From the days of John the Baptist until now, the kingdom of heaven suffers violence, and the violent bear it away." Though this is one of Jesus' more mysterious sayings, the meaning of "the violent" is simple enough. We cannot sit and wait for heaven, for God's reign of peace, to fall into our laps. We must go after it zealously. As Thomas Cahill puts it, "the passionate, the outsized, the out-of-control have a better shot at seizing heaven than the contained, the calculating, and those of whom the world approves." Interestingly, the Christian vocabulary is not alone in using violent language to describe the way of peace. According to a Muslim source, the word *jihad* does not only mean the holy war of Islam, but also the spiritual battle that takes place within each of us.

Many Christians today disdain the idea of spiritual warfare. For one thing, they feel it is a figment of the imagination; for another, they feel the language used to describe it is too confrontational, too in-your-face and, worst of all, too old-fashioned. Yet the cosmic fight between the angels of God and the hosts of Satan continues to this day, despite dwindling belief in its reality. Why should we presume it is an abstraction just because we don't see it?

I believe that the invisible powers of good and evil are every bit as real as the physical forces that make up our universe, and unless we are able to discern them, we cannot enter into the vital battle that takes place between them. As light cannot share space with darkness, so good and evil cannot coexist, and we must, therefore, decide which side we will take.

In 1975, as senior elder of our congregation, my father drew up a document we have turned to repeatedly over the years. A "covenant" signed by all members of our community at the time it was written (and still affirmed by every new member), it has often helped us to sharpen our focus on the roots of a particular problem we are grappling with.

We declare war against all irreverence toward the childlike spirit of Jesus.

We declare war against all emotional or physical cruelty toward children.

We declare war against the search for power over the souls of others.

We declare war against all human greatness and all forms of vanity.

We declare war against all false pride, including collective pride.

We declare war against the spirit of unforgiveness, envy, and hatred.

We declare war against all cruelty to anyone, even if he or she has sinned.

We declare war against all curiosity about magic or satanic darkness.   (*excerpts*)

One of the greatest risks in taking up arms against evil is to mistake the battle for something that must be fought on a human level, between opposing camps of "good" people and "evil" ones. We may speak of God and the church in contrast to Satan and the world, but the reality is that the dividing line between good and evil runs through every human heart. And who are we to judge anyone but ourselves?

Gandhi once advised, "If you hate injustice, tyranny, lust, and greed, hate these things in yourself first." Each of us creates an atmosphere around himself. As we "fight the good fight," let us not forget to pause, now and then, and ask ourselves whether this atmosphere is one of fear, or of the love that casts out fear.

It is tempting to carry out the fight in others rather than in ourselves. Horrified at the state of the world or at other people's lives, we may become filled with a righteous (if not self-righteous) zeal. But rather than winning others over to a new life, or finding their hearts, we may end up distancing ourselves from them. The battle must be waged in our own hearts first.

Glenn Swinger, a fellow minister, wrote to me in this regard:

> After experiencing conversion, I was baptized in my mid-forties…I confessed every instance of sin I could think of, cleared up wrongful relationships with other people, and tried to see how deeply I had opposed God. I felt forgiveness, which brought joy and peace. Yet your father, who baptized me, said, "Now the real fight begins." I'm not sure I

really understood this at the time, but I told myself I would be watchful.

Little by little, however, I slipped back into old ways, and slowly the little devils of pride and envy and jealousy reentered my life. The experience of baptism certainly changed me, I won't deny that. Yet I did not conquer self. I remained all too much the center of my inner experiences. I was living a wonderful life in my own strength, with my own capabilities. I did not "watch and pray" that temptations would not enter my heart...Eventually the first love that had drawn me to Christ was shattered.

Later my hypocrisy was revealed, and I experienced the pain of judgment. I was asked to lay down my service as a minister and teacher. I moved away from my community for four months, during which time I was able to face my sins squarely and repent. Coming back and receiving the forgiveness of the same brothers and sisters I had separated myself from, I found new freedom, love, and peace.

Struggles still come every day, but over the years I am slowly learning something of what 1 Corinthians 13 means: after all else is said and done, there is only faith, hope, and love; and love is the greatest. I cannot judge or look down on another, no matter what his condition. The rich man created a chasm between himself and Lazarus, and in the hereafter their positions were reversed. There are two mighty forces at work in each of us, evil and good, and in the battle between them we are judged and forgiven over and over. It is in this – in the ongoing fight – that we experience true peace.

Glenn's observation is crucial to understanding the paradox above, "I came not to bring peace, but a sword," for it touches on its deepest meaning. Christ's sword is his truth, and we must allow it to cut us deeply and repeatedly whenever sin crops up in our lives. To harden ourselves or protect ourselves from it is to close ourselves to God's mercy and love.

The Violence of Love

If genuine peace demands warfare, then it also demands blood, and not only in a figurative sense. Christ forbids us to use force against others, but he clearly demands our readiness to suffer at the hands of others. He himself "bought us peace through his blood," as the New Testament says, and down through the centuries thousands of men and women have followed his example and willingly given their lives for their faith.

The significance of dying for one's convictions may be one of the hardest things to explain. Most of us shudder just imagining the gory spectacle of people being burned, drowned, even torn apart. Yet eyewitnesses have written again and again of the remarkable peace shown by martyrs in their last moments.

In *The Chronicle of the Hutterian Brethren*, a Reformation-era history that includes accounts of many martyrdoms, we read of people who went to their deaths singing joyously. In one, Conrad, a young man about to be executed, remained so purposeful and calm that onlookers said they wished they had never met him, he made them so uneasy.

For most of us, martyrdom seems an unlikely end. We are rarely called on to defend our faith even verbally, and the idea of paying for it physically seems overly dramatic. All the same, it never hurts to consider the faith of those who are ready to suffer for their beliefs—and to ask ourselves if we would be prepared to do the same. Anyone can control his emotions enough to remain composed in the face of day-to-day hardships. Yet for peace to remain in the face of serious struggle or even death, it must be rooted in more than good intentions. Somewhere, there must be a deeper reservoir of strength.

Salvadoran Archbishop Oscar Romero touched on the secret of this peace when he spoke, shortly before his death, about the importance of accepting the "violence of love." Romero was assassinated in 1980 because of his outspokenness on behalf of the poor.

> The violence of love...left Christ nailed to a cross; it is the violence we must each do to ourselves to overcome our selfishness and the cruel inequalities among us. It is not the violence of the sword, the violence of hatred. It is the violence of brotherhood, the violence that will beat weapons into sickles for peaceful work.

Christ's love, then, is a force for truth and holiness, and attacks by its very nature all that is unholy and opposed to truth. It is an utterly different love from that preached by many spiritual leaders of our culture, such as popular New Age author Marianne Williamson, who suggests that in order to find peace, all we need to do is to love ourselves as we are and "accept the Christ who is already in us."

Not surprisingly, most of us prefer her teaching. We know that every Christian has a cross to bear, but beyond that we would rather not deal with the issue. We prefer the warm, friendly religiosity of the modern church, and the goodwill promised by the angels at Bethlehem, to the hard-won peace of Golgotha. We admire Jesus' yieldedness as he died—"Father, into thy hands I give my spirit"—but tend to forget his agonizing struggle to find it during the long, lonely night before, in Gethsemane. We prefer the resurrection without the crucifixion.

Recently a verse in the Book of Jeremiah struck me: "Is not my word like a fire, like a hammer that breaks the rock in pieces?" God can only be referring to the hardness of our human hearts. Normally we think of hardness in the way it shows itself in a criminal: in a murderer, rapist, adulterer, or thief. In counseling prison inmates, however, I have found that the most violent criminal may have the softest heart, because he is the most conscious of his sin. How I wish I could say the same of others I have counseled—"good" people with well-fed egos and carefully constructed images. Perhaps the greatest hardness is in those who are burdened by these things.

Even when we are aware of our shortcomings and struggles, we often resist the violence of love. We seek genuine, lasting peace and know it will cost us something, but before long we settle for less. A young man in my congregation once said to me, "I've struggled and struggled to find peace, but then I ask myself, 'Why are you putting yourself through this hell? Is it really worth it?'" Naturally I could not answer this question for him. But looking back, I might have asked him a question in return: What is peace worth to you, if it is not worth fighting for?

Uncanny as it sounds, those who are surest they do not possess peace are sometimes the closest to finding it. Robert (not his real name) is a convict "doing life" at an upstate prison. He committed a horrible crime, and there are times when he is so tortured by the memory of what he did that he can hardly stand the thought of living another day. At other times, his remorse has given him a sense of peace. In a recent letter he wrote:

> You asked if I could write something about peace, the peace of God. I would love to, but I don't think I am qualified to do so. I don't feel qualified because I feel that the peace that you are talking about has eluded me almost my entire life.
>
> I've searched for peace in many ways: through women, my grandmother, achievements, drugs, and sometimes violence and hate; through sex, marriage, children, and money and possessions. In none of these things did I find any peace.

It's weird, though. I never experienced peace, but I know what it is and what it feels like. I describe it as being able to breathe, and rest. All of my life it felt (and still feels most times) like I'm suffocating or drowning and in a constant struggle to breathe and rest.

I long for such a peace. I've learned...that the only way I can get this peace is through Christ, and still it eludes me. I am not at peace, because of what I did and what it did to others. I am so sorry.

I pray for a second chance at life, beyond man's prison of steel and concrete and Satan's prison of sin. Knowing that God can bring this about is where my faith and hope has been, and still lies.

To have God finally answer my prayers even after all the pain, unrest, and struggles in the past would bring me such a peace. So would knowing that someone loves me in spite of who I am and what I've done, and forgives me enough for that second chance...

Robert sounds almost hopeless in his letter, but I (and others who have visited him) have noticed a definite change in him since his arrest three years ago. It is not that he has "arrived"; nor could one honestly say that he has found peace. But Robert hungers for it. And because he is going through the agony of true repentance, he may be closer to God than many of us.

In a passage on peace in an ancient Hindu text, the *Bhagavad Gita*, it says: "Even murderers and rapists...and the most cruel fanatics can know redemption through the power of love, if they but yield to its harsh but healing graces. Passing through excruciating transformations, they shall find freedom, and their hearts shall find peace within them." And in the Letter to the Hebrews we read, "No hardship or discipline seems pleasant at the time, but painful. Later, however, it produces a harvest of righteousness and peace for him who has been trained by it." Robert may not be familiar with either text. Yet as he struggles, he is experiencing their truth. He is living the violence of love.

No Life without Death

As I worked on this book, two sayings of Jesus in the Gospel of John especially deepened my understanding of peace: "Unless a kernel of wheat falls to the ground and dies, it remains only a single seed. But when it dies, it produces many seeds." And: "The man who loves his life on this earth will lose it, yet the man who loses his life for my sake will have eternal life."

In the same way that there is no lasting peace without struggle, there is no true life without death. Because we are not faced with imminent death, we lose sight of this important fact. We forget that, to understand the peace of Jesus, we must first understand his suffering. The willingness to suffer is important, but it is not enough. Suffering must be experienced. As my father once put it, "To experience even a little taste of godforsakenness is decisive to the inner life."

To most of us, godforsakenness might seem a negative thing that has nothing to do with peace. It means pain, not pleasure; suffering, not happiness; self-sacrifice, not self-preservation. It means loneliness, denial, alienation, and fear. Yet if we are to find any meaning in life, we must be able to find it in these things. Suffering, as the great Jewish psychiatrist Viktor Frankl has pointed out, "cannot be erased from the palette of life. Without it, human life would not be complete."

Many people spend their lives trying to escape this truth; they are some of the most unhappy souls in the world. Others find peace and fulfillment in accepting it. Mary Poplin, an American who spent time with the Missionaries of Charity in Calcutta in 1996, says of them:

The Missionaries look at trials and insults as times for self-examination, to build humility and patience, to love their enemies – opportunities to become more holy. Even illness is often interpreted as a way of coming closer to God, as a way of God revealing himself more clearly, and as an opportunity to discern problems in one's own character more profoundly.

We spend a great deal of time in our lives trying to ease and avoid suffering, and when it comes, we do not know what else to do with it. Even less do we know how to help others who suffer. We fight it, assign blame to individuals and social systems, and try to protect ourselves. Rarely do any of us consider how suffering might be a gift from God, to call us to become more holy.

While we often say that crises and times of suffering build character, we avoid both whenever we can, and expend much effort creating techniques to compensate for, minimize, or overcome the suffering. In fact, much of our secular literature suggests that Mother Teresa and the Missionaries are psychologically flawed in their acceptance of pain and suffering. Having worked alongside them, I think nothing could be further from the truth. We Americans are rarely encouraged to take responsibility for our own suffering. Yet regardless of the situation, each of us has at the very least choices to make about how we respond to suffering.

To the Missionaries, suffering is not merely a physical experience, but a spiritual encounter, one that encourages them to learn new responses, to seek forgiveness, to turn to God, to think like Christ, and to rejoice that the suffering has produced a good work in them. It is, finally, a spur to action.

Equally significant is the witness of people like Philip Berrigan, who have not only accepted suffering in their lives, but embraced it. Phil knows more about losing one's life "for my sake" than most Christians in our day. For him, answering Christ's call to a life of discipleship has meant persecution in the form of one jail sentence after another. In the 1960s he and his brother Daniel were arrested for protesting the Vietnam War, and since then he has spent a total of eleven years behind bars.

I visited Phil in a Maine prison where he was being held for the latest of his numerous acts of civil disobedience. A few weeks later he was sentenced to two years in prison—two years of separation from his wife, Elizabeth McAlister, and their three children. It was not the first time they had been separated. But neither Phil nor Liz were disheartened. In a touching letter she wrote to him, Liz reflects on the basis of their peacemaking, which has often been misunderstood and criticized for its political overtones but reveals an unflagging optimism and faith:

> It isn't fair—at age seventy-three you are looking for the umpteenth time at a jail sentence for justice' sake and for peace. And that you face it without even a hearing in the court. But what else can we expect when millions are in prisons around our world, so many of them under torture, starving, disappeared, their loved ones bereft?
>
> It isn't fair—we can't enjoy the home we built together; admire, as they bloom, the roses we transplanted; eat the fruits we've nurtured; take pride in the children we've raised. But what else can we expect when millions are homeless, millions more are refugees of war, famine, repression—their souls too dazed by weariness and fear to see the beauty around them; their hopes and hearts so broken by the daily dying of their children...?
>
> It isn't fair—we can't celebrate Frida's and Jerry's college graduations together. They long for you to be with them and partake in their pride, accomplishments, new beginnings. They long for your wisdom, your heart, your presence in this new phase in their lives. But what else can we expect when for the vast majority of kids a college education, a loving family,

a caring community isn't even the stuff of dreams, victims as they are of the decrepit institutions that pass for public education, victims too of the futurelessness that is the great society's legacy to them?

It isn't fair—we can't guide Kate together as she looks to high school graduation and beyond, as she becomes a young woman...

It isn't fair—the community you've worked all these years to build and rebuild is without you, the prayer and work and dreaming and laughter devoid of your special gifts and vision and grace. But what else can we expect when community of any sort is suspect, a threat, an aberration, when the silence is almost complete, when people are cowed, bought off, distracted, participants in their own extinction...?

The sense of peace and purpose that flows from people like Liz and Phil is neither prized nor understood in our society. It is a fruit of the paradoxical freedom of Christ, who says, "Though no one takes my life from me, I lay it down of my own accord. I have the power to take it up again."

To Phil, a sacrifice such as separation from his loved ones is par for the course—part of the death that must be suffered on the road to peace. It has not brought him peace as the world gives, but as he wrote from prison, his eyes are on a far greater, deeper peace:

It is that peace where domination is no more, where injustice is undone, where violence is a relic of the past, where swords have disappeared and plowshares are abundant. It is the peace where all people are treated as sisters and brothers, with respect and dignity, where each life is sacred, and where there is a future for the children. It is such a world that God calls us all to help make a reality.

In our country this can mean going to jail, risking reputation, job, or income, and even being disowned by family or friends. Yet, in a criminal state which daily prepares for nuclear holocaust, it truly means freedom, a sense of self and vocation, and a whole new community of friends and family. In fact, it means resurrection.

For most of us, the dying we must undergo in order to bear fruit is fairly mundane. Instead of facing a firing squad (like Dostoevsky) or a federal judge (like the Berrigan brothers), we face little more than the hurdles of daily living: overcoming pride, yielding to someone who has wronged us, letting go of a resentment, submitting to an angry or frustrated family member or colleague. There is nothing heroic in choosing to do these things. But "unless the seed be buried" we will never find true peace or be able to pass it on to others.

Laurel Arnold, a member of my church whom I have known since the late 1950s, says:

> When I think of the words of Jesus in John 14 – "My peace I give to you, not as the world gives" – I remember how often these verses were read at funerals but remained outside of me.
>
> I grew up in a protected and lonely environment to become a righteous, pious, critical woman. I wanted to be somebody, maybe a famous writer, and worked hard to get honors in college. I longed to be popular, yet judged classmates who were. I was idealistic about pacifism, but I was so terribly middle-class white, and blind to social injustice and power politics.
>
> I spent the war years teaching in New York City, while Paul, my husband, was at sea. After the war, we began to wake up to the realities of other people's lives. Paul had seen the terrible destruction of bombed cities in Europe; I'd stepped over drunks on the street and cared for children who never played on grass. We thought we could help an alcoholic by including her in our family, but she stole our grocery money.
>
> We offered ourselves to our church mission board and were sent to Africa. Though we later left the mission field, we

became more and more involved in church activities. But we never found the heart-to-heart relationships we were looking for, because of all the superficiality and gossip. We wanted to live a life of following Jesus every day, not just on Sundays.

Later, feeling drawn to the ideal of brotherhood, we began to examine issues and areas of our life we hadn't thought of before: materialism, private property, the causes of war. In 1960 we came to the Christian community where we still live, which practices full sharing. Giving up the house and car and pooling our goods was easy; it made sense to us. But opinionatedness, principled ways of reacting to things, self-righteous judging; bossiness, and being so sure of oneself that it crushes others – those things were harder. For a long time I struggled against acting by rules instead of by the Spirit, against being "good" or "nice" when genuineness or honesty was needed.

Of course there have been as many joys as struggles and the faithfulness of God over all these years, reaching out to judge and forgive and grant the possibility of a new beginning. I still don't like to be wrong – no one does – but I have found such grace, such love in God's judgment. At seventy-four, there is no time to relax and get cozy. There is still so much to learn, so much to respond to…

Some people thank God in their prayers that they are his children. I'm not so sure as that. Am I really ready to die? Certainly I don't live "serenely," like it says in a song we sing, "Peace I ask of thee, O river." There is a certain restlessness and longing in me. I guess we're all part of the groaning creation mentioned in Romans 8. When I look at myself I get shaky, but when I think how faithful God has been all through my life – there is my trust and my peace.

There is nothing special about Laurel's story. Yet the normalcy of her struggle – the universal, life-long task of learning to live in peace with God, our neighbors, and ourselves – makes it no less important than the most heroic martyrdom. My grandfather writes:

43

As far as humankind as a whole is concerned, only one thing is worthy of the greatness of God's kingdom: our readiness to die. But unless we prove this readiness in the trivialities of daily life, we shall not be able to muster courage in the critical hour of history. Therefore we must overcome completely all our petty attitudes and feelings, in order to give up all our personal ways of reacting to things, that is, our fear, worry, inner uncertainty—in short, our unbelief. Instead, we need faith: faith small as a tiny seed, but with the same potential to grow. This is what we need, neither more nor less.

The Wisdom of Fools

In his first letter to the Corinthians, the apostle Paul writes, "Do not deceive yourselves. If you think that you are wise in this age, you should become fools so that you may become wise. The wisdom of this world is foolishness with God." The wisdom of fools (and the foolishness of the wise) may not seem directly related to peace, yet as a central biblical theme it sheds light on an important aspect of our book. If God's peace is not peace as the world gives, then it cannot be found by those who follow the world's wisdom, but only by those who embrace the foolishness of God.

On a practical level, this foolishness is often derided or dismissed. The story of Francis of Assisi is a case in point. Today he is best known as a harmless monk who wrote songs to the sun and made peace with animals and birds. Yet St. Francis was no mild-mannered poet. A passionate soul, he sought to identify with the poor by giving up not only his inheritance, but even the clothes from his back. His last will and testament was so unsparing in its criticisms of wealth and institutional religion that it was confiscated and burned before he was deemed "safe" for sainthood. And the few words he left us reveal a depth of spirit that should challenge us every time we read them – never mind how trite they have been made by overuse.

> Lord, make me an instrument of thy peace!
> Where there is hatred, let me sow love;
> Where there is injury, pardon;
> Where there is doubt, faith;
> Where there is despair, hope;
> Where there is darkness, light;

And where there is sadness, joy.
O divine Master—
Grant that I may not so much seek
To be consoled, as to console;
To be understood, as to understand;
To be loved, as to love.
For it is in giving that we receive,
In pardoning that we are pardoned,
And in dying that we are born to eternal life.

Those who bristle at accepted "religious" answers today, like St. Francis seven centuries ago, are just as likely to be scoffed at. Like him, they may find that the road to lasting peace demands the willingness to be misunderstood and misrepresented.

In my book on death and dying, *Be Not Afraid*, I told the story of my aunt Edith, who traded a comfortable lifestyle as a theology student at Tübingen University for the poverty of an obscure religious order. Edith's "foolishness"—Hitler was in power, and the order had been denounced as a threat to the State—angered her parents so much that they locked her in an upstairs bedroom and refused to give her food until she changed her mind. (She made a rope of sheets and escaped through the window.)

Marjorie Hindley, a vibrant English member of my church, met resistance of a different sort, but underneath the tensions were the same:

> I grew up attending the Methodist Church, though later I became an Anglican. When my siblings and I were small, my mother always prayed with us at bedtime. There was an accepted standard of conventional morals in the family.
>
> Father was socialistic in his thinking, and I shared his strong desire for justice. Mother, however, was much more conservative, and my brother responded to that line of thinking, so we were often at loggerheads.

As an adolescent I never really lost faith in the Christian teaching, but I struggled to find what it meant. I was about sixteen when my thinking was first jolted: a cousin of one of my classmates had taken a stand as conscientious objector to war, and was imprisoned. That was a shock, and from then on I began questioning things and wanting to know what the Christian teaching was. I remember protesting loudly at home one day about the injustice of something, and my mother said, "Wait till you lose your illusions." I told myself fiercely, "I am not going to lose them," but later I began to wonder: are they merely illusions, or are they the real thing, and the rest of life an illusion?

Marjorie worked as a secretary, first in Manchester and then at Cambridge University. It was a comfortable job: short hours, long holidays, and a pension to look forward to in forty years' time. She held out for about two years, but then left, feeling, "there must be something more to life than this." Later she studied industrial psychology. After short stints at several different factories, she found a permanent position as a welfare supervisor with a firm in Bristol.

I had gone into this work with the conscious desire to make myself useful, to help solve the need of the world in some small way, to live a more "Christian" life. Yet I found more questions than answers. The workers were warmhearted and supportive of each other; the forewoman less so; the directors agonized over their need to show good profits. Was it the workers who needed my help, or the directors? The workers were giving me more than I could give them. If I was looking for fulfillment, what did fulfillment mean for them? What had happened to that fire of the first apostles, who got up and followed Jesus? What was Christianity and the peace of Christ really all about?

I hid a New Testament in my office drawer and read it during the lunch hour with my door locked. I discovered the Sermon on the Mount, and pondered it.

I went to one church or the other on Sundays, and to the
Folk House, a youth center, on weekdays. Once I stood outside the vicarage door and wondered if I should ask to talk
with the vicar. But I retreated without asking. Another time
I was walking along the road in great frustration, and I heard
a voice speak so clearly that I looked round to see who was
there. No one was there, but the voice had said, "It will not
be long now."

Around the same time I discovered that one of the directors where I worked was a Quaker, and I asked him if I could
borrow any of his books. He brought me George Fox's
Journal, and *Studies in Mystical Religion* by Rufus Jones.
They were a great help to me. In the evenings, at the Folk
House, I met with other young men and women who were
concerned about the issues of the day. War was looming on
the Continent. What stand were we to take? Why did the
churches give no clear leading?

Eventually, Marjorie's seeking led her away from the
sources of conventional religious wisdom – away from the
Quakers who gave her books but could not answer her questions; away from the Church of England, which cheered
its bishops on when they wrote dramas about peace, but
refused to stand behind them when they spoke out against a
brewing conflict with Germany. During a visit to our community, she says, it became clear to her what she must do.

Suddenly, in the midst of the poverty and the scrubbing and
the vegetable cleaning, I knew what I had to do: I had to begin
again. I had to give up everything I knew to be wrong and
dedicate my life to following Jesus. The light that dawned on
me was amazing – it was a discovery of joy, of conviction, of
peace.

Marjorie became a member, though she would be the first
to protest if her story were taken to mean that one must

join a church in order to find peace, let alone a specific community or congregation. Her belief in Christ's call to radical discipleship is unflagging, however. As she has advised dozens of young men and women over the years, true peace of mind comes from following one's heart, "no matter how strong the opposition of your parents, employers, colleagues, friends, and even your church."

Complacency often blinds us to the real issues of life. Materially and spiritually, we feel so satisfied with the wisdom of our culture that we never bother to rouse ourselves inwardly, not even to raise basic questions like the ones Marjorie asked. At best this is unfortunate, because it robs us of the chance of experiencing the peace that is gained through searching for our own answers. At worst, it is religious blindness, if not madness. Novelist Annie Dillard writes:

> On the whole, I do not find Christians, outside of the catacombs, sufficiently sensible of conditions. Does anyone have the foggiest idea what sort of power we so blithely invoke? Or, as I suspect, does no one believe a word of it? The churches are children playing on the floor with their chemistry sets, mixing up a batch of TNT to kill a Sunday morning. It is madness to wear straw hats and velvet to church; we should all be wearing crash helmets. Ushers should issue life preservers and signal flares; they should lash us to our pews. For the sleeping God may wake someday and take offense, or the waking God may draw us out to where we can never return.

The Strength of Weakness

I have often thought that the most difficult of Jesus' paradoxical sayings—at least in terms of putting it into practice—might be the verse in Matthew where Jesus has just noticed a child. He turns to his disciples and tells them, "Whoever humbles himself like this child is the greatest in the kingdom of heaven."

To become like a child means to unlearn almost everything society has taught us about growing up. It means overcoming our temptation to look strong. It means being willing to be hurt, rather than protecting ourselves. It means recognizing that we have limitations and weaknesses, and humbly coming to terms with them.

Christ healed the sick, fed crowds, turned water into wine, and walked on water. He had every source of strength at his command. But when he was arrested, brought before Pilate, mocked, scourged, and crucified, he refused to defend himself. And he did not choose to be born in a palace, but in a humble stable.

Christ chose the "weakness" of submission, and perhaps that is a hidden key to his peace. Dorothy Day writes:

> We are told to put on Christ, and we think of him in his private life, his life of work, his public life, his teaching, and his suffering life. But we do not think enough of his life as a little child, as a baby. His helplessness. His powerlessness. We have to be content to be in that state too. Not to be able to do anything, to accomplish anything.

Gertrud Wegner, a family friend, was forced to accept this state when an accident left her unable to move:

> I was at a business exhibit with my husband in Washington, D.C., and I fell and severely injured my spinal cord. I knew

right away that I was in critical condition; I had no feeling anywhere, and from my neck down I was completely paralyzed.

Two operations helped significantly, but the hours of therapy – two routines a day – meant hard work and perseverance. It was exhausting. And my doctor did not even know if I would gain back any ability to move at all...My accident taught me humility, because every little thing had to be done for me. Month by month one could see little improvements, but it was a long, uphill struggle. There were hard moments, yet I also learned to accept my weakness. I tried to remember what Paul says: "Christ's strength shows itself in the most glorious way through our weakness."

There have been other personal battles, but in each one my longing for peace, and faith that I would find it again, has held me through. It seems that if you have had peace once in your life, it comes back to you again and again.

Thinking back over my life, many things come to mind. I wish I had been a better mother to my children. I wish I had spent more time with my father when he was dying of cancer. I wish I had shown more love to my mother, especially at that time, and supported her more. I wish I had been kinder to others...There are so many things you wish you could do over and do differently, but that doesn't help. The only thing we can do is to accept our limits and make a fresh start each day.

My peace comes in hoping to serve Jesus and my brothers and sisters until the last minute of my life, though I know that would be a special grace and presumptuous to ask for. The older I get, the clearer it is to me that none of us "have it." Our peace is undeserved.

Gertrud's thoughts touch on a significant truth: the more confidence we have in our own strength and abilities, the less we are likely to have in Christ. Our human weakness is no hindrance to God. In fact, as long as we do not use it as an excuse for sin, it is good to be weak. But this acceptance of weakness is more than acknowledging our limitations. It means experiencing a power much greater than our own, and surrendering to it.

> This is the root of grace: the dismantling of our power. Whenever even a little power rises up in us, the Spirit and the authority of God will retreat to the corresponding degree. In my estimation this is the single most important insight with regard to the kingdom of God. *Eberhard Arnold*

Kathy Trapnell, another member of my church, attests to the truth of these words in her life and search:

> The quest for peace was in me since I was old enough to sense unpeace in my own family, and there was plenty of that in a big way. Throughout my Catholic schooling (from first grade through four years of college) there was always the struggle for peace in myself and among friends. When a good little Catholic sees where she went wrong and feels sorry, the next thing is to go to the box to make a good confession. How vividly I remember the unmistakably happy feeling I got as a school girl after every such confession! Even in college, once or twice, I made what is called an "open" confession to a Jesuit I knew well, and the feeling of being right with God was a source of peace.
>
> But then came the rebellion of my student years, my hippie phase, which I was proud of, and my anger against the status quo and everything in it that I thought worked against peace and love. I imagined I was making peace – by seeking to end the Vietnam War, by marching, singing, supporting war resisters, and so on. I thought I could bring some fairness to the plight of the migrant workers by boycotting grapes and causing chaos in the local supermarkets that carried them. I tried to share everything I had; I did yoga, pooled my money with others, and learned to be happy in a commune.
>
> None of it really brought me peace. I now think the reason I found no peace was because the bottom line, my orientation,

was wrong. Not that these things weren't or aren't good causes. But I was my own god; I was the standard by which I judged my life and other people's lives. I was frightfully, sinfully, willfully my own boss, and I tried to do everything in my own strength. It doesn't work.

Later I discovered an entirely different spirit of peace—the peace of a faith that takes our weaknesses for granted, confronts them, and points us to Jesus—to the kingdom, God's future reign of peace. This recognition judged me. I saw how selfish I was, and that I was actually a very unpeaceful person. But in surrendering my life to God—not only to his love, but to his judgment—and giving myself in service to others, I have found a new strength, and daily miracles of peace.

Everything in our society gravitates away from Kathy's understanding of peace. We are taught to take judgment as an affront, to stay in control. All of us are for peace and love; not one of us would deny that they are good things. But to stop and ask ourselves whether we have found them in our own hearts is quite a different matter. It's not something you talk about.

Perhaps that is why so many of us who look for peace do not find it. We are too concerned with our role in the search. We lack humility and simplicity, and instead of turning to Jesus to ask him for his peace, we worry about our integrity in other people's eyes. We forget that the Beatitudes do not call for great saints who shine before men, but for lowly people.

Writer Henri Nouwen, who left an illustrious career at Harvard, Yale, and Notre Dame to serve the handicapped, understood this as few others have:

> We have been called to be fruitful—not successful, not productive, not accomplished. Success comes from strength, stress, and human effort. Fruitfulness comes from vulnerability and the admission of our own weakness.

For a long time, I sought safety and security among the wise and clever, hardly aware that the things of the kingdom were revealed to little children; that God has chosen those who by human standards are fools to shame the wise. But when I experienced the warm, unpretentious reception of those who have nothing to boast about, and experienced a loving embrace from people who didn't ask any questions, I began to discover that a true spiritual homecoming means a return to the poor in spirit, to whom the kingdom of heaven belongs.

What motivates a person to seek such poverty of spirit? My grandfather writes:

It amounts to a clash between two opposing goals. One goal is to seek the person of high position, the great person, the spiritual person, the clever person, the fine person, the person who because of his natural talents represents a high peak, as it were, in the mountain range of humanity. The other goal is to seek the humble, the minorities, the handicapped and mentally retarded, the prisoners: the valleys of the lowly between the heights of the great. They are the degraded, the enslaved, the exploited, the weak and poor, the poorest of the poor. The first goal aims to exalt the individual, by virtue of his natural gifts, to a state approaching the divine. In the end he is made a god. The other goal seeks the wonder and mystery of God becoming man, God seeking the lowest place among men.

Two completely opposite directions. One is the self-glorifying upward thrust. The other is the downward movement to become human. One is the way of self-love and self-exaltation. The other is the way of God's love and love of one's neighbor.

When a person has been given the peace that comes from living in this love, there is nothing he cannot face. Think of Jesus on the cross. Here is the ultimate vulnerability, but also the supreme example of God's peace. In spite of all that was done to him, he had no self-pity, but turned and forgave one of the criminals next to him. He was able to say of his persecutors, "Father, forgive them, for they do not know what they do." And there is Stephen, the first Christian martyr, who knelt and looked to heaven with a radiant face while being stoned to death. He too said, "Father, forgive them." I do not believe such peace can be attained by human strength.

Stepping Stones

"It is little by little that we proceed."
Paul the Apostle

Stepping Stones

Thomas Jefferson was so convinced that the pursuit of happiness was an inalienable human right that he wrote it into the Declaration of Independence and called it a self-evident truth. But Christians have this to add: those who pursue happiness never find it. Because joy and peace are extremely elusive, happiness is a will-o'-the-wisp, a phantom, and even if we reach out our hand to grasp it, it vanishes into thin air. God gives joy and peace not to those who pursue them but to those who pursue *him* and strive to love. Joy and peace are found in loving and nowhere else.   *John Stott*

Hard as it is to accept, the presence of peace in our lives may have little to do with how earnestly we seek it. It is simply a fact that peace sometimes eludes those who run after it the farthest, whereas those who may not even be looking for it—in some cases, people who have never given the issue a second thought—stumble across it as if by chance. At the same time, the Bible contains dozens of verses such as 1 Peter 3:11, which tells us to turn away from evil and do good, and try to live in peace "even if you must run after it to catch and hold it."

The question of whether we should or shouldn't actively pursue peace can never be fully resolved. Peace is a vast theme, and to address it in big, sweeping statements is no help to anyone. Neither is chasing grand solutions, such as trying to save humankind or bring about world peace. Most of us have no lack of commitments to fulfill right on our doorsteps—small ones, perhaps, but ones that need our attention today. That is why I believe Stott's words may contain another key to peace: instead of pursuing it for its own sake, we should look for it in active loving. Paul suggests the same in his Letter to the Romans: "Make every effort to do what leads to peace." Each of us can love, and each of us can surely find, somewhere in our lives, something we can do that leads to peace.

Naturally, before we do anything, we must choose to do it. The words of Jesus, "My peace I leave you; not as the world gives do I give to you," hold out a promise. But they also invite us to make a choice. We can receive the peace Jesus offers, or turn our backs on it and seek instead the peace the world gives. It is one choice among many, but I would venture to say that it is by far the most crucial one, because its ripples will be felt in every sphere of our life, and every other choice we make—economic, personal, political, and social—will be affected by it sooner or later.

Even Jesus was faced with choices. After his baptism in the Jordan by John the Baptist, the Spirit led him into the desert, where he was to be tempted by the devil. He fasted for forty days and forty nights, and afterward, at his weakest and most vulnerable, he found himself cornered and presented with a decision: to take the "easy way out" and to give in to Satan's scheming, or to stand strong on the side of God.

In the course of a lifetime each of us must undergo hours of temptation, even if none of them will be as agonizing. But Jesus' decisiveness in choosing to remain true to his Father—and the victory this brought about—should give us hope and strength. It should also remind us that we are all called to be children of God.

God has sown goodness.
No child is born evil.
We are all called to holiness...

Why then is there so much evil?
Because the inclinations of the human heart
have corrupted people, and they need purification...

No one is born to kidnap,
no one is born to be a criminal,
no one is born to be a torturer,
no one is born to be a murderer.
We have all been born to be good,
to love one another,
to understand one another.

Why then, O Lord, have so many
weeds grown up in your field?
The Enemy has done it, says Christ,
and the people, who have let the weeds
grow in their hearts...

Youth: ponder how we are all called to goodness,
and how the older generation—my own, I regret—
has left you a legacy of so much selfishness
and so much evil.

Renew, new wheat, newly sown crops,
fields still fresh from God's hand.
Children, youth: be a better world.

Oscar Romero

Growing up I was fortunate to have parents who encouraged me to (in Romero's words) "ponder how we are all called to goodness." For them, Christ's promise of peace was no mere verse in scripture, but a real offer that they were determined to take up. Neither Papa nor Mama were saintly. They hated pretense and false piety and sometimes irked others with their down-to-earth manner. Yet no one who knew them will deny that they tried to match their deeds to their words, and that their joy in life was serving God and others.

When Papa spoke about the peace of God, it was always in the same context: he told us that it was only given to people who were detached from earthly things. "Where your treasure is, there is your heart." His father, a well-known writer and lecturer in Berlin who left his career for a life of Franciscan poverty, told his children when they were still young that he would not leave them a monetary inheritance; his gift to them would be the example of a Christ-centered life.

My parents left me the same legacy, though I didn't always appreciate it. In fact, I consciously rebelled against it in my early teens. Not that I did anything scandalous by today's standards: I knew what my parents' values were and more or less wanted them for myself. I was also aware of the sacrifices they had made to follow God. (My mother had left a prestigious boarding school against the wishes of her family, who hoped she would become a professor, and it had taken years for the tensions to be resolved.) But first I wanted to have fun. When there was a choice, that usually meant going along with my peers, even if it hurt my parents.

Then God stopped me in my tracks. I was fourteen, and our family had just moved from our community in the backwoods of Paraguay, where I had grown up, to Woodcrest, our new settlement in New York. At the time of our arrival in the United States, there seemed to be a general air of optimism — the economy was booming, and the glow of American "victory" over Germany and Japan had not yet faded. All the same, the Cold War was in full swing, and many people feared nuclear disaster. At least in the circles my parents moved, people were turning away from the hollow triumphs of wealth and war and looking for something new: simplicity, community, harmony, peace.

From the day we arrived at Woodcrest I was exposed to this searching. There were hundreds of guests (mostly young) and dozens of new members from every imaginable background, and their questions got me thinking as never before. Here were men and women who had been "making it" in worldly terms yet had chosen to throw it all away in exchange for a life devoted to God. Here were people who were voluntarily selling houses and cars and giving up good jobs to become poor. I could tell by their faces and words that it brought them fulfillment and joy. Soon the things I had hankered after seemed less important, and my plans for life after high school—college, money, and adult independence—began to change. After a while they even seemed petty and insignificant. I had new goals and priorities.

It is hard to pinpoint the most important event that altered the direction I was headed in. I still remember the day I told my parents of my decision to live differently—for God, and not for myself—from now on. I am not sure if I would speak of it as a definitive "conversion." But it was one of several important experiences that strengthened my longing to find a true purpose in life, and it deepened my conviction.

Books, especially the novels and short stories of Tolstoy and Dostoevsky, helped shape my thinking, though I was not so conscious of it then. I was a voracious reader, but I did not regard their books as "religious" material. Conversations with guests such as Dorothy Day and Pete

Seeger had a great impact on me too. Looking back, I also realize the role my parents played, though I was not aware of this either—at least not until I saw their tears when I told them about my change of heart. They must have prayed for me often, and hard.

Perhaps the most important factor in those years was my father's influence as a pastor. Watching Papa baptize others always struck me. I sensed a spirit of holiness, of God, and this sense was confirmed later, when I saw the transformation in those he had baptized. Some people changed so entirely, they seemed to have taken on a new personality. I wanted the same for myself—to make a complete break with my self-centered struggles, and to find the joy and freedom of a new beginning. When at eighteen I was baptized, it was a decisive event: I now knew there could be no turning back from dedicating my life fully and forever to God.

Earlier in this book I quoted a rabbi who suggested that peace must be built "brick by brick." The image is a good one. A conversation, a book, an experience that moves us inwardly (even if we are not able to explain why), a decision—by themselves, none of these will necessarily change the course of our lives. But together they build on each other and make us who we are. Ultimately they are the things that either prevent us from finding peace of heart, or lead us to it.

I have met people who could tell me the exact moment they were converted, and how it happened, and I do not doubt their sincerity. But most of us probably identify better with the late British writer Malcolm Muggeridge. He writes:

> Some, like the apostle Paul, have Damascus Road experiences, and I have often myself prayed for such a dramatic

happening in my own life that would, as it were, start me off on a new calendar, like from B.C. to A.D. But no such experience has been vouchsafed me; I have just stumbled on, like Bunyan's Pilgrim.

For me, too, conversion was not a step but a process. First there was my yearning for something new, then my decision to start living for others, and then baptism. Today, over forty years later, I am still asking new questions and finding new answers. Here again the image of stepping stones comes to mind.

Each of the following sections offers such a foothold. Not all of them are smooth or safe. Some, like humility and trust, involve risks and may even turn out to be stumbling blocks. Yet along the path to peace, each of them must be crossed.

Simplicity

The object of life is not to be on the side of
the majority, but to escape finding oneself in
the ranks of the insane...Remember that there
is a God who desires neither praise nor glory
from men created in his image, but rather that
they, guided by the understanding given them,
should in their actions become like unto him.
The fig tree is true to its purposes, so is the dog,
so also are bees. Is it possible, then, that man
shall not fulfill his vocation? But alas, these
great and sacred truths vanish from memory.
The bustle of daily life, war, unthinking fear,
spiritual lameness, and habitual servitude stifle
them.   *Marcus Aurelius*

For most of us the desire for peace does not come from some
noble search to be one with God, though this yearning may
grow along the way. Usually it is set into motion by something much simpler: dissatisfaction with the daily stress
and strain in our lives, and the fear that – as Aurelius puts
it – we are going insane.

Our culture is not only marked by frenzy, but driven by
it. We are obsessed (to quote Thomas Merton) with our
lack of time and space, with saving time, with conquering
space, with making conjectures about the future, and "worrying about size, volume, quantity, speed, number, price,
power, and acceleration." We live, he continues, in "the
time of no room, which is the time of the end."

We are numbered in billions, and massed together, marshaled, numbered, marched here and there, taxed, drilled, armed... nauseated with life. And as the end approaches, there is no room for nature. The cities crowd it off the face of the earth. There is no room for quiet. There is no room for solitude. There is no room for thought. There is no room for attention, for the awareness of our state.

Worse, we do not merely lack peace – time, space, room – for ourselves; we prevent each other from finding it.

In the last twenty-five years alone, new inventions and improvements have utterly transformed the way we live. Computers and other hi-tech labor-saving conveniences have revolutionized our work and home life. Yet have they brought us the peace and freedom they seemed to promise?

Without realizing it, we have become dulled, if not brainwashed, in our eagerness to embrace technology. We have become slaves to a system that presses us to spend money on new gadgets, and we have accepted without question the argument that, by working harder, we will have more time to do more important things. It is a perverse logic. When upgrades on everything from software packages to cars keep us on the constant run; when we are always struggling to keep up with the Joneses (even against our better judgment), we ought to ask ourselves what we have saved, and whether our lives are any more peaceful.

If anything, the increasing complexity of life today has only robbed us of peace and resulted in a quiet but widespread epidemic of nervousness, insecurity, and confusion. Already fifty years ago German educator Friedrich Wilhelm Foerster wrote:

> More than ever before, our technical civilization has cushioned life on all sides, yet more than ever, people helplessly succumb to the blows of life. This is very simply because a

merely material, technical culture cannot give help in the face of tragedy. The man of today, externalized as he is, has no ideas, no strength, to enable him to master his own restlessness and division. He does not know what to make of suffering—how to make something constructive of it—and perceives it only as something that oppresses and exasperates him and interferes with his life. He has no peace. And the same experiences that might help a person with an active inner life gain mastery over life may be enough to send him into a mental institution.

In a recent "trends" item, *Time* reported on a young couple who moved away from their wealthy Ohio suburb because the woman was sick of living in a neighborhood where people "spend all their time working their backs off so they can fill their big, empty houses with expensive crap." She wanted "serenity, simplicity, some peace of mind."

At first, life in their new small-town surroundings seemed perfect, but before long, joblessness pushed the crime rate up, and trouble with narrow-minded neighbors brought headaches. Determined not to give up, the woman threw herself into historic real-estate renovation and school board issues. This didn't seem to bring fulfillment either. Finally the couple hit on a great plan for achieving the serene lifestyle: they headed off to Nantucket to start a bed-and-breakfast...

Like happiness, simplicity cannot always be had by being chased. That is not to say it is an invalid search. But to pursue it for its own sake may only end in disappointment. If we are disillusioned with a materialistic lifestyle and want to escape its clutches, more will be required of us than a change of pace.

In my parents' youth in Europe during the 1920s, the search for a simpler life was combined with a longing for genuineness, reverence for nature, community, and harmony with the Creator. Like the youth of the sixties, young people of my parents' day formed cooperatives where they could live closer to each other and—though most shied away from religious language—closer to God.

Today, voices like Wendell Berry (Kentucky's "Thoreau") emphasize the importance of returning to nature, learning to become more self-sufficient, and "living simply so that others may simply live." In southwestern France, Thich Nhat Hanh's Plum Village, a retreat center and community of predominantly Vietnamese monks, nuns, and families, has much to say about the relation of simplicity and peace.

Those of us who have young children (or grandchildren, nieces, or nephews) should not forget that their simplicity has important things to teach us too. Unlike adults, children tend to embrace the essential and immediate. Their greatest pleasure is in natural and simple things. They live more fully in the present and act more readily from the heart, because their minds are freer of plans, schemes, inhibitions, and motives.

Simplicity cannot be an end in itself. Nonetheless it remains something we must strive for continually when possessions and activities and agendas distract us from the important things of life—family, friends, constructive relationships, and meaningful work. These are the things that connect us and draw us together. We ought to spend more time with our children and less with our tools and toys; to become less dependent on things and more dependent on God.

Christ asked, "What does it profit a man if he gains the whole world, and loses his own soul?" I have often turned to this simple question and found peace in it. It is not a threat held over our heads, but a sure guide, and a reminder of our true priorities.

Silence

The tongue is our most powerful weapon of manipulation. A frantic stream of words flows from us because we are in a constant process of adjusting our public image. We fear so deeply what we think other people see in us that we talk in order to straighten out their understanding. If I have done some wrong thing (or even some right thing that I think you may misunderstand) and discover that you know about it, I will be tempted to help you understand my action.

Silence is one of the deepest disciplines of the Spirit, because it puts the stopper on all self-justification. One of the fruits of silence is the freedom to let God be our justifier. We don't need to straighten others out.

Richard J. Foster

One of the greatest hindrances to peace is our inability to be silent. For every situation in which we decide to hold our tongue or mind our own business, there are others where we let our heads be turned and join the chatter. We are constantly robbing ourselves of peace, because we choose to meddle in the affairs of others. We talk. We gossip. And we forget that for every idle word, we will be judged.

Silence may not seem like a "big deal" in comparison with other aspects of peace addressed in this book. Writer

Max Picard points out that silence "stands outside the world of profit and utility. It cannot be exploited; you cannot get anything out of it. It is 'unproductive'; therefore it is regarded as useless. Yet there is more help and healing in silence than in all the useful things."

When we are alone, outward silence is easy to cultivate. (Inwardly, we may not be quiet at all; our head may be buzzing with ideas and plans.) When we are with others, it becomes more difficult. It involves more than not talking – it means learning to listen.

At my community, where evening meetings for worship, business, reading, or informal sharing are held several times a week, one might think we know the value of silence. Perhaps we do. But it is amazing how our desire to express ourselves, to voice our opinions and to make ourselves heard, can get in the way of fruitful dialogue.

Not to react, not to revise or embellish or expound, not even to respond, but simply to *listen* is a gift. When we are able to be truly silent, to truly listen, then God can speak. This is a discipline. Mother Teresa points out that what we have to say is never as essential as what God says to us and through us: "All our words are useless if they do not come from within. Words that do not carry the light of Christ only increase the darkness."

Many people seem to regard silence as a trapping of an unnecessarily severe life – something for monks or nuns, for "religious" people. It is true that in many religious orders, members practice silence. In our community, a vow of silence may be taken for a short period by someone who wishes to reaffirm his or her commitment, or as a sign of penitence. But why should it be seen in a negative light? Silence can relieve us of the burden of having to respond. It can help us to avoid getting flustered over petty things.

Among the early Friends (Quakers), worship and ministry took second place, after the practice of common silence, which they saw not as an end in itself, but as a way of "waiting on God." Friends felt that because silence drew one away from the self and into a greater sphere, it was the most fruitful state in which to find consensus and unity, even on a divisive issue. When talking and searching and praying led nowhere, silence could enable them to hear the Spirit and find an answer.

> Silence before God has deep significance: in the quietness of the soul the individual sinks into the central fire of communion. In the circle of worship the most personal elemental chords of life receive their deepest stimulation...In the silent act of breathing and in the unspoken dialogue of the soul with God, solitary as these are, deep communion can be given.
>
> *Eberhard Arnold*

Sometimes silence requires physical solitude. If we live or work closely with others – in a close-knit family or community, for instance – it is especially necessary to find times to be quiet and alone. Bonhoeffer says that those who cannot live in community cannot live with themselves, but the reverse is also true. Those who cannot live with themselves cannot live in community. To quote my grandfather again:

> Just as we breathe in and breathe out, we need solitude to gain strength for the times when we are with others. We know from Nietzsche's life of Zoroaster that the ancient prophet was often alone with his animals. He went out and walked silently among these intelligent, strong, noble, yet submissive beasts, and through this he regained his strength and felt driven once more toward men.

Personally, I think it is important to make time for solitude every day, even if only for a few minutes. My wife and I

Free Book offer

- To give to colleagues, friends or relatives
- Request larger quantities for free* distribution at events.
- Display for people to pick up at work, school or church.

Please send me books as marked to the right:

Name

Organisation

Address

Address

City _____ Post Code

E-mail or Telephone number (mandatory)

Or request your books on

E-mail: contact@ploughbooks.co.uk

Free phone: 0800 018 0799

Quantity

Rich in Years
Finding peace and purpose in a long life. Rediscover the spiritual riches that age has to offer.

Quantity

Seeking Peace
Draws on the wisdom of some exceptional (and some very ordinary) people who found peace in surprising places.

Quantity

Be Not Afraid
Deals with uncertainty, loss, grief and the fear of death and dying.

Quantity

Their Name is Today
Addresses current issues that threaten childhood and suggests creative ways to help children, families and teachers.

Quantity

Why Forgive?
Stories of people who overcame scars left by violent crime, interpersonal strife and their own failures.

View our full list of titles at **www.plough.com**
*Donations are appreciated. Cheques payable to Plough Publishing

Plough
PLOUGH PUBLISHING HOUSE

Freepost Plus RTHT-UBYG-KTXK
Plough Publishing House
Darvell
Brightling Road
ROBERTSBRIDGE
TN32 5DR

take a quiet walk in the morning as often as we can, and find it a good way to focus our thoughts. Others in our community do this too: one elderly couple takes a short walk before dinner every day, simply to be quiet together and enjoy the evening. Especially when we are going through a period of turmoil or loss, the silent, healing power of the outdoors should not be underestimated. I can still hear Ria Kiefer, an elderly woman of my childhood days, telling someone who looked sad, "*Freu' dich an der Natur!*" – Go out. Enjoy nature!

In his book *Freedom from Sinful Thoughts* my father writes about another kind of silence – detachment, or inner quiet. There is plenty that could be said about detachment; the mystics have written whole volumes on it. Yet it can also be defined very simply as the peacefulness that comes from dropping everything that occupies our minds – the clamor of work, the distraction of plans, our worries about tomorrow – and becoming inwardly still. Seventeenth-century Quaker William Penn explains why this is so important:

> Love silence even in the mind; for thoughts are to that as words to the body, troublesome. Much speaking, as much thinking, spends; and in many thoughts, as well as words, there is sin. True silence is the rest of the mind, and is to the spirit what sleep is to the body, nourishment and refreshment. It is a great virtue; it covers folly, keeps secrets, avoids disputes, and prevents sin.

All of us know what it is like to sit with someone we love, not saying anything yet feeling perfectly at ease. But silence is not always a source of peace. Sometimes a slight pause in a conversation is enough to unsettle us, and we grope for a quick reply to bridge the uncomfortable gap. When things are not right inside—when there is something between us and another person, or between us and God—silence can even be frightening.

A woman I have counseled for several years tells me that during times of upheaval, she finds peace by dropping everything and becoming silent inside:

> It seems that when you are not at peace with yourself, you will have a hard time coping with blank spaces, either visually (nothing to watch or read), auditorily (nothing to listen to or hear), or physically (nothing to do, or the inability to do anything). You try to keep yourself distracted from the trouble inside—pain, conflicting goals, fear, accusations, a bad conscience, whatever—but you only become more flustered. However much you avoid blank space, you can find a blessing in it when you accept it and use it to the soul's good. Facing inner turmoil is hard, but it can ready you for the gift of peace, and for a life more in tune with God's will.

Sophie Loeber, a childhood friend of my father's whom I have known all my life, recently wrote to me in a similar vein. "I have often had to fight for peace in my life," she says, "but silence helped me turn inward and remember that God holds each of us in his hand."

Sophie was among the members of our German community that was raided and dissolved by the Gestapo (secret police) in 1937. After rounding them up, lining the men against a wall, and locking the women and children in a room, the police interrogated them and announced that they had twenty-four hours to leave the premises and get out of the country.

> When the Nazis forced us to leave our beloved home in the Rhön, we were not allowed to take anything with us other than the clothes on our backs. But we carried our treasures—joys and sorrows, struggles and times of celebration,

and everything we had experienced there over many years—in our hearts. No one could take those from us, even if we were utterly stripped of all material goods. That filled me with a silent joy and brought peace to my heart.

Many years later Sophie and her husband, Christian, lost two sons to a rare disease. First the boys went blind; then they became mentally debilitated. Both died in their teens, only a few years apart. Sophie was stricken beyond words. Questions tortured her, but gradually they gave way to a silence in which she found faith—and peace:

> Again and again I asked myself: why is God sending us this terrible trial? Sometimes the discouragement seemed too much to bear, even when we turned to God...Yet later, in times when I was able to collect my thoughts and become inwardly silent, I realized that my concerns and prayers were much too small, too personal. Christian and I had been circling around our own needs, forgetting that there were people right next door who had needs too. We had also forgotten the promise, "Seek first the kingdom of God, and everything else will be added unto you."

More recently, Sophie lost her husband to cancer, and then a third son (married, with children) in an electrical accident. God has surely tested her, but she says her suffering has taught her to become inwardly quiet and to "let go of everything that binds us here on earth." Through this she has been able to make room for God and "let him fully into my heart, and my wounds have begun to heal."

> Now that I am nearing the end of my life, silence has become even more important to me. "Be still and know that I am God." Everything needs to fall away so that God can fill us completely. Then we will experience true joy, and we will find peace.

Surrender

Difficulties should not depress or divert us. The cause that has gripped us is so great that the small weaknesses of individuals cannot destroy it. Therefore I ask you only one thing: do not be so worried about yourself. Free yourself from all your plans and aims. They occupy you far too much. Surrender yourself to the sun, the rain, and the wind, as do the flowers and the birds. Surrender yourself to God. Wish for nothing but one thing: that his will be done, that his kingdom come, and that his nature be revealed. Then all will be well. *Eberhard Arnold*

The best way not to experience peace of mind is to focus continually on ourselves. To look inward, to sort out motives, to ask ourselves questions we have blocked from our minds for fear of change – all these are a necessary part of examining the roots of unpeace. But to stop there is death. Turning inward is not the same as turning to God. Once we have weighed our problems, we must surrender them to God and move on. The sooner we do this, the sooner we will know peace.

Some people seem inclined to watch themselves constantly, as if in a mirror, and because of this they are unnecessarily tense. Others may not be so conscious of their inner state but are just as tense because they cannot let go of old hurts. With one it may be a smoldering resentment; with another an unfulfilled desire or an unconquered frustration.

Winifred Hildel, a member of my community, went through a period of deep grief after her only son was stillborn. Unable to let go of her loss, she clung to the idea that she must have done something wrong to bring it about, even though her doctor assured her this could not have been the case. Only years later was she able to stop torturing herself. By sharing the full details of everything she imagined she had done wrong, she was able to let go of her self-accusations.

Winifred's long inner conflict points to a source of unpeace that causes many people heartache: their attempt to come to terms with a tragedy they feel responsible for. Whether or not they objectively bear guilt, the key to resolving it is surrender. Humility is a virtue, but self-recrimination is not. It does not bring healing but leads to unhealthy introspection.

For some, another source of unpeace is their inability to relinquish the control they try to exert over others. In my work providing pastoral counseling for families, I have seen how crippling this can be in the home, especially when it defines the relationship between a parent and child. In many homes, a great deal of unpeace, especially between older teens (or even adult children) and parents, could be solved if parents were able to let go of their child and place his or her future in God's hands. My mother, a teacher, used to tell parents, "The greatest disservice you can do your children is to bind them to yourselves. Let go of them. Bind them to God."

Emotional bondages create tensions outside the home, too, especially in workplaces, churches, and social organizations. The tendency to meddle, advise, or criticize others runs countless people to a frazzle and makes life miserable for everyone around them.

Perhaps the most widespread cause of unpeace is simply our self-will—our insistence on directing the course of our personal lives. To want to call one's own shots is natural, but it leaves no room for God. If we want his peace in our lives, we must let him do the leading, whether things are running smoothly or we are going through rough times. We need to mean it when we pray, "Thy will be done."

In connection with my writing and speaking work I have met Molly Kelly, a mother, author, and public lecturer, several times. Molly is best known for her expertise in teen sexuality, but she has valuable insights on the search for peace of mind, too—and the role of surrender in finding it.

I grew up in a Catholic family with five brothers and a sister, and Mom and Dad loved us very much. Not everything always went right, but love was the glue that bound us together. I went off to college...and met the love of my life: Jim, a handsome young medical student at Georgetown. Jim and I started to date when I was a sophomore, and we married the year after I graduated. Ours was a marriage made in heaven, as they say. He loved me, I loved him, and because of our love for each other we decided to allow God to be our family planner. And what a generous God he is. We were blessed with eight children in eleven years!

But what about peace? When I think of the word, I think first about how much people bandy it around and misuse it...

One day twenty-two years ago my life changed forever. Jim and I were away for the weekend with three couples who were our best friends. It wasn't easy to get away because of Jim's schedule at the hospital, and because of our eight young children. So we were very excited. We were going to spend the weekend at a winter resort in the Poconos. But let me now fast-forward you to the event that catapulted me into an unrest and sadness that permeated every fiber of my being and remained there for years, until I let God come and set me on my journey toward peace and joy.

I was at the top of a sled run, chatting with our friends, when I noticed a commotion at the bottom of the slope. Jim had just gone down the hill on the sled, but I hadn't watched him so I didn't know it had anything to do with him. I saw several people waving to us, and I wondered what was going on. Then someone yelled for me to come down quickly because Jim had been hurt. I ran the whole way down the hill, slipping and falling and getting up again, and when I arrived at the scene there was a crowd around Jim. They stepped aside and made room for me, and I knelt at his side. He was semiconscious and bleeding profusely. I'll skip the details and get to the end. Jim died.

I was devastated. Jim was my best friend, my pillow-talk buddy, the father of our children, the builder of our dreams. I couldn't begin to fathom life without him. I will never forget going home and hugging each one of the children, who had already been told that their dad had died. Our eldest, Jim, was twelve, and our youngest, Dan, was fourteen months. The older ones were pale, sad, and clinging to each other. The younger ones weren't sure what was going on. The house was filled with people, noise, and lots and lots of food. (It's interesting how people bring food to console a grieving family.) God was compassionate and shielded and surrounded me with family and good friends, and I was grateful for the outpouring of love, but I was too hurt to thank anyone. I was wounded and bleeding just like Jim, and no one could fix my wounds either, so they seeped and festered for years.

I was able to go on as far as taking care of the kids because I loved them so much, and because I promised myself I would never dishonor Jim's memory by doing a shabby job of raising our children. I still had two in diapers, and because children want things to be better quickly, the rest of them went back to playing football in the living room, making a playhouse out of my couch cushions, and making demands on my time and patience. Time I had; in fact it weighed heavily on me, even though I never seemed to get done all that I had to do. Each day dragged on, and I couldn't wait for bedtime so I could go to sleep and forget for just a little while that Jim had died. I was short on patience.

I was never alone, yet I was lonely beyond belief. It was only later, when peace came, that I discovered the difference between loneliness and being alone. I still dread loneliness, but I have come to cherish times when I am alone with myself and God.

Some time after her husband's death, Molly took up an issue that had concerned him greatly: abortion. As a Catholic physician who believed in the sacredness of all life, Jim was an ardent opponent of *Roe v. Wade*, and Molly felt the same as he did, although she had never stated this publicly.

I had never spoken in public before, and I was scared to death to do so now, but I said to myself, "You've survived the worst – Jim's death. How bad can public speaking be?"

I began by addressing the issue in classes at local Catholic high schools, and within a few years I was speaking quite a bit. I arranged my schedule so that I would be home when the kids got back from school in the afternoon.

After a while I realized that I wasn't getting to the heart of the problem. I realized I needed to talk about the root of abortion, which had to do with unwanted pregnancies, which had to do with casual sex. So I began to speak about sexual responsibility, which I call chastity. That was the beginning of a resurgence in teaching abstinence, and the invitations to speak came pouring in. I was asked to speak in so many schools and so many other venues that I became overwhelmed and didn't know where to turn.

Friends suggested that I cut down on my speaking, but I felt God had called me to this mission of public speaking, and I wasn't about to give it up. Still, something had to give. It was then that I realized that what had to give was *me*. I had to give it all over to God, to surrender, and I wasn't used to that.

I liked to be in control. I was the mother of eight children, and I ran a tight ship. I bought the food, I made the dinners, I washed the clothes, I helped with the homework, I went to the plays and ball games, I was home and school president. The word "surrender" was not in my vocabulary. What I didn't realize was that surrender to God does not mean giving up so much as it means giving over. I had to give over my control, my unrest, my loneliness, my being overwhelmed – even my children – to God. And in each area of my life where I was able to do this, the tangible peace I experienced was almost instantaneous.

One thing that happened was a new awareness of the Holy Spirit, for the first time since my confirmation. I had grown up praying to God and picturing Jesus, but the Holy Spirit was just someone who flew in and out for the occasion of my confirmation. In surrendering myself to God (and let me say here that it takes a daily effort) I began to realize that Pentecost, the descending of the Spirit into our lives, is an ongoing happening.

Molly has spoken to more than a million teens – "my favorite people in the whole world" – and to thousands and thousands of parents. She has addressed a gathering of six thousand priests in Rome, and a meeting of fifty cardinals and bishops in California.

My schedule can be overwhelming, but it no longer overwhelms me. My peace is deep. It's a serenity that seems to have settled in for the long haul, for as long as I keep renewing my surrender to God. I say yes to speaking engagements when I can and when I think God wants me to, and I say no when I can't. Am I always right? I doubt it. But I have confidence in knowing that God never takes away his gift of peace if we continue to give our lives to him, even when we fail now and then...

I have come to realize that it is only in surrender that true peace will come. Surrender in war means losing, giving up. Surrender to God is winning and giving over your life to him. I start out each day at Mass asking God to help me be him to everyone I meet during the day and, even more important, to see him in everyone I meet. But then I get out my white flag that only God can see and boldly wave it back and forth, letting God know that today I am surrendering, once again, to his will. It's a daily exercise that firms up my spiritual life; and believe me, he always gives me his joy and peace.

Countless people struggle on bravely, even when they feel burned-out, simply because they are not willing to let down their guard before God. They are determined to steer their own lives, cost what it may. Such people over-commit and then take days off to recuperate. They work at balancing their schedule, at discerning their priorities. They pray, they work hard, they try to be humble and loving at home and forbearing at work. At the end of the day they still have no real peace.

Recently someone asked me how I keep my balance from day to day. "Don't you go insane worrying over all the souls in your care?" Serving as a pastor is always challenging, and as senior elder of a church of 2,500 there are many times when I feel inadequate. Thankfully I have the support of a dozen or more fellow pastors in guiding the congregations I am responsible for, and there is also my loyal wife. Still there are days when anxiety clouds the horizon. Sometimes, humanly seen, a situation looks utterly hopeless.

It is just at moments like these, when we feel the greatest danger of losing our equilibrium that God can give us inner assurance and peace – if we turn to him. Once we surrender our problems and our need to solve them our way, we will find that the highest hurdle is no longer insurmountable.

We are promised this in the Psalms: "Cast thy burdens upon the Lord, and he will sustain thee." To the modern mind this seems too simple, too good to be true. But for those who believe, it is an offer God always makes good.

Christoph Friedrich Blumhardt, the late-nineteenth-century "father of religious socialism" and pastor of a large parish, is said to have gone to bed peacefully every night while his wife Emilie stayed up worrying. Rankled by his ability to pray for their parishioners, turn over, and fall asleep, Emilie asked her husband the secret. "Is God so powerless that my worrying would help the well-being of the parish?" he answered. "There comes a moment each day when we must simply drop everything that weighs on us and hand it over to God."

Even with the best efforts, our strength is minuscule, and our solutions patchy. Surrender means recognizing the incomparably greater power of God, and giving him room to work in our lives.

It helps now and then to step back and take the long view. The kingdom is not only beyond our efforts. It is even beyond our vision. We accomplish in our lifetime only a tiny fraction of the magnificent enterprise that is God's work. Nothing we do is complete, which is another way of saying that the kingdom always lies beyond us. No statement says all that could be said; no prayer fully expresses our faith. No confession brings perfection; no amount of pastoral care brings wholeness. No program accomplishes the church's mission. No set of goals and objectives includes everything.

This is what we are about: we plant the seeds that one day will grow. We water seeds already planted, knowing that they hold future promise. We lay foundations that will need further development...

We cannot do everything, and there is a sense of liberation in realizing that. It enables us to do something small, and to

83

try to do it well. It may be incomplete, but it is a beginning, a step along the way, an opportunity for the Lord's grace to enter and do the rest. We may never see the end results, but that is the difference between the master builder and the worker.

We are workers, not master builders; shepherds and sheep, not messiahs. We are prophets of a future not our own.

attributed to Oscar Romero

Prayer

The effect of prayer is union with God; and if someone is with God, he is separated from the enemy. Through prayer we guard our chastity, control our temper, and rid ourselves of vanity. It makes us forget injuries, overcomes envy, defeats injustice, and makes amends for sin.

Through prayer, physical well-being, a happy, peaceful home, and a strong, well-ordered society are obtained. Prayer shields the wayfarer, protects the sleeper, and gives courage to those who keep vigil. It will refresh you when you are weary and comfort you when you are sorrowful.

Prayer is the delight of the joyous, and the solace of the afflicted. It is intimacy with God and contemplation of the invisible. Prayer is joy in things of the present, and the substance of things to come. *Gregory of Nyssa*

There are times when nothing will give us peace but prayer. We may strive for simplicity and silence – for detachment from sources of unpeace around us or inside us – but we may still be left with a void that only God can fill. And if he does not enter our hearts uninvited, we must ask him to come in.

In Psalm 130, one of my favorites, the line "Out of the depths I cry to thee" sheds light on how we should pray in times of need. Actually, it reflects the spirit in which we should always turn to God: we are always in the depths, in need of his help and guidance, and he is always there above us, firm and secure and strong.

The Jewish philosopher Martin Buber says that whenever we pray, we should cry out, imagining ourselves as hanging from a cliff by our hair, with a tempest raging around us so violently that we are sure we have only a few seconds left to be saved. Buber goes on, "And in truth there is no counsel, no refuge, and no peace for anyone save to lift up his eyes and his heart to God and to cry out to him. One should do this at all times, for a man is in great danger in the world."

Buber's image is dramatic, but it is not exaggerated. In a culture like ours, where the long arm of the mass media reaches so far that news of celebrity, scandal, or catastrophe can stop millions of people in their tracks, the individual has never been so susceptible to the lure of following the crowd. Nietzsche saw this a hundred years ago when he mused on the truth of the old proverb, "*Gemeinschaft macht gemein*" – "community makes common (crude)" and warned of the dangers of a society where mass-values are so strong that they can deaden even the strongest conscience.

Without an active prayer life we lose strength of character and succumb to what sociologists call herd instinct: we fall prey to fear of others, to ambition, to the desire to please people. Without prayer, the constant traffic and opinions of people around us will swamp our inner lives and finally drown them. We think we are our own masters, but in actual fact many of us cannot think for ourselves, let alone pray, anymore. Having lost its relation to God, our life consists merely (to quote Nietzsche again) of "constant adjustments to all sorts of different collective influences and societal demands."

As a protective armor around the quiet flame of the heart, prayer is the best defense in the face of such onslaughts. And it is more: it is a life-giving discipline that can bring us to our senses—back to God—when we have gone astray. It focuses us and directs us to the source of peace.

Personally I have found the discipline of prayer crucial to maintaining a sense of peace and order in my life. More than anything else it seems that prayer (or the absence of it) can decide the outcome of our day. As Bonhoeffer notes in his *Letters and Papers from Prison*, time we waste, temptations we yield to, laziness or lethargy in our work—in general, any lack of discipline in our thoughts or in our interaction with others—frequently have their root in our neglect of prayer.

Prayer need not be formal. For my wife and me, it is the natural way we begin and end our day together; we pray every morning when we get up, and every evening before we go to bed. Some may pray more often than that, others less. Some people pray on their knees; others use a prayer book. Some speak; some do not use words at all. Pastor Blumhardt, whom I referred to earlier in this book, was known to open his window each evening in order to say good night to God. As long as our prayer is genuine, and not just an empty rite, it does not matter how we go about it. The important thing is to make room for it, somewhere.

In the turmoil of life without, and black despair within, it is always possible to turn aside and wait on God. Just as at the center of a hurricane there is stillness, and above the clouds a clear sky, so it is possible to make a little clearing in the jungle of our human will for a rendezvous with God. He will always turn up, though in what guise and in what circumstances cannot be foreseen—perhaps trailing clouds of glory, perhaps

SEEKING PEACE

as a beggar; in the purity of the desert or in the squalor of
London's Soho or New York's Times Square.

Malcolm Muggeridge

Alongside Muggeridge's thoughts stands the biblical command to "pray without ceasing." For many who seek God,
the idea is simple enough. Molly Kelly says, "Prayer used
to be when I would talk to God at certain times of the
day—in the morning, or before I went to bed. Now I know
that it is an all-day conversation with God. I pray as I walk
through the airport or down the supermarket aisle."

For others, this way of thinking is an obstacle. How does
one pray all day? What does "unceasingly" mean? James
Alexander, an old friend of mine, pondered this for years:

Although I have prayed ever since I can remember, it was
only when I began to understand prayer as a way of life—as
a constant attitude rather than a repetitive action—that I
understood the idea of praying without ceasing. The Prayer
of Jesus as explained in *The Way of a Pilgrim*—"Lord Jesus
Christ, have mercy on me, a sinner"—was helpful too. The
book says that if there is one thing we can offer God, it is the
constancy of such a prayer. But it is not merely a group of
words. It is an attitude to life.

Nineteenth-century poet Gerard Manley Hopkins says
much the same:

It is not only prayer that gives God glory, but work. Smiting
on an anvil, sawing a beam, whitewashing a wall, driving
horses, sweeping, scouring, everything gives God some
glory if being in his grace you do it as your duty. To go to
communion worthily gives God great glory, but to take food
in thankfulness and temperance gives him glory too. To lift
up the hands in prayer gives God glory, but a man with a
dung fork in his hand, a woman with a slop pail, give him

88

glory too. He is so great that all things give him glory if you mean they should. So then, my brethren, live.

Each of us will pray differently. And as our circumstances change – through illness, old age, or crisis, for instance – so may our prayer life.

Doug Moody, a member of my church, found little meaning in prayer as a young man. Upset by the hypocrisy he perceived in his mainstream denomination, Doug found himself increasingly at odds with the church of his youth, especially on the issue of military service, which he opposed as a conscientious objector to war. After the bombing of Pearl Harbor, classmates and teachers at the University of North Carolina praised his refusal to be conscripted, but his church did not. The judge who tried and sentenced him as a felon for evading the draft was a member of his own congregation.

There I sat in an antiquated county jail, with crab lice, awful food, a broken shower, and no issue of clothes. Fortunately, my mother was able to bring me soap and a change of underwear. It was the first, hardest period of my sentence, and was lightened only by listening day after day to the story of an utterly broken German alien on his way to an internment camp. A neighbor had falsely accused him of espionage.

In prison I read in the FOR magazine *Fellowship* that the Mennonite couple who had inspired me not to register had changed their position. I was angry. But there was a strange blessing on my imprisonment: slowly, through my little bit of suffering – the endurance of tedium and filth, and our treatment not as men but as numbers – I was led to take an interest in this needy inmate in the next bed, and the joy that comes from living for others began to waken in me.

I began to see what Thomas Kelly meant by living in the "eternal now," for every inmate was constantly talking about the time left until his release, forever living in the future. When I began to live in the moment—not for release, not even for the next meal or movie or chance to sleep—it became possible for me to be at peace even in prison.

Years later, during a difficult period of struggle in his personal life, Doug found new meaning in prayer. "In place of all the usual ways to escape discouragement or depression, prayer—in the simple sense of turning to God and my neighbor in love—became the foundation for a lasting peace and a purpose in living." Now, as he enters old age, Doug says that his personal prayer life has taken on an importance it never had in earlier years.

> Regular prayer with my wife, or alone—morning, noon, bedtime, and when I lie awake at night—has become a lifeline, the only help in the face of the inevitable failures, temptations, discouragements, or periods of depression that each of us goes through at one time or another.
>
> It is not always a matter of words. Part of it is a quiet turning toward God throughout the day, an upward glance, a moment or two of silence remembering someone who is sick or suffering or struggling. Part of it might be considering various concerns and questions of the day. Part of it is asking for light to see my wrongs, to recognize where I might have hurt others. Prayer helps me strengthen my commitment to Christ and to my brothers and sisters. In all of this there is peace—not as the world gives, but the peace of Jesus.

Karl Barth once wrote that to clasp one's hands in prayer is the beginning of an uprising against the disorder of the world. If this is true, and I believe it is, then our prayer life cannot exist in a separate sphere, and our prayers must consist of more than longings or intentions. Just as faith without deeds means spiritual deadness, so prayer without work is hypocrisy. Even without deeds, our prayers must be more than self-centered pleas for personal happiness if they are to have any effect on the rest of the world.

Doug hints at the importance of including others in our prayers. Among the early Christians and down through the history of the persecuted church and its martyrs, we find the same thought, and an even more radical one—the practice of praying, as Jesus commanded, for those who persecute us. We must be ready to do the same for those who hurt us, whether through backbiting, slander, or anything else.

If we claim to love our enemies but then fail to pray for them, we deceive ourselves. *Sojourners* founder Jim Wallis writes:

> As long as we do not pray for our enemies, we continue to see only our own point of view—our own righteousness—and to ignore their perspective. Prayer breaks down the distinctions between *us* and *them*. To do violence to others, you must make them enemies. Prayer, on the other hand, makes enemies into friends.
>
> When we have brought our enemies into our hearts in prayer, it becomes difficult to maintain the hostility necessary for violence. In bringing them close to us, prayer even serves to protect our enemies. Thus prayer undermines the propaganda and policies designed to make us hate and fear our enemies. By softening our hearts towards our adversaries, prayer can even become treasonous. Fervent prayer for our enemies is a great obstacle to war and the feelings that lead to war.

Numerous prayers are said in times of war or national crisis, but they are rarely offered up in this spirit, at least not publicly. I remember an occasion during the Gulf War, right after the United States launched a full-scale ground attack on Iraq in early 1991. Addressing the nation over network television, President Bush implored viewers to drop whatever they were doing and pray for "our boys" in the Gulf. He ended his speech with a fervent "God bless the United States of America."

Most of us probably stopped and fulfilled our patriotic duty without further thought. Yet as Thich Nhat Hanh has pointed out, there were probably equal numbers of Iraqi Muslims bowing to Allah just at that moment, sending up prayers on behalf of *their* husbands and sons. How could God know which nation to support?

People pray to God because they want God to fulfill some of their needs. If they want to have a picnic, they may ask God for a clear, sunny day. At the same time, farmers who need more rain might pray for the opposite. If the weather is clear, the picnickers may say, "God is on our side; he answered our prayers." But if it rains, the farmers will say that God heard their prayers. This is the way we usually pray.

In the Sermon on the Mount, Jesus taught, "Blessed are the peacemakers: for they shall be called the children of God." Those who work for peace must have a peaceful heart. When you have a peaceful heart, you are the child of God. But many who work for peace are not at peace. They still have anger and frustration, and their work is not really peaceful...

To preserve peace, our hearts must be at peace with the world, with our brothers and our sisters. When we try to overcome evil with evil, we are not working for peace. If you say, "Saddam Hussein is evil. We have to prevent him from continuing to be evil," and if you then use the same means he has been using, you are exactly like him. Trying to overcome evil with evil is not the way to make peace.

When you pray only for your own picnic and not for the farmers who need the rain, you are doing the opposite of what Jesus taught. Jesus said, "Love your enemies, bless them that curse you." When we look deeply into our anger, we see that the person we call our enemy is also suffering. As soon as we see that, we have the capacity of accepting and having compassion for him. Jesus called this "loving your enemy." When we are able to love our enemy, he or she is no longer our enemy. The idea of "enemy" vanishes and is replaced by the notion of someone suffering a great deal who needs our compassion. Loving others is sometimes easier than we might think, but we need to practice it. If we read the Bible but don't practice it, it will not help much.

Thich Nhat Hanh

Trust

Trust the physician, and drink his remedy
in silence and tranquility:
For his hand, though heavy and hard, is guided
by the tender hand of the Unseen,
And the cup he brings, though it burn your lips,
has been fashioned of the clay which the Potter
has moistened with his own sacred tears.

Kahlil Gibran

From childhood on we are taught that it is dangerous to trust, and in a way this is true. To trust involves taking risks. Trust means giving others the benefit of the doubt. It requires the willingness to make oneself vulnerable. It means knowing that our security is in a higher power, and that our peace will not stand or fall on our ability to hold everything together. Trust is yielding to God in faith.

Contrary to popular opinion, trust is not the same as weak-willed naiveté. It does not require us to go through life unperturbed and happy, pretending that nothing is wrong and taking everything at face value. Such "trust" would be suicidal in today's climate. Yet the alternatives — anxiety, mistrust, and suspicion — are equally deadly. Mennonite writer Daniel Hess notes:

> It does not matter that many workers are covered by health insurance, that the forty-hour work week provides time for leisure, that salaries give some of us a degree of affluence, and that science goes a long way in making tools safe and in predicting volatile nature. In spite of all that, we are anxious.
>
> People have tight stomachs and sweaty palms because of learned habits of nervous busyness, fear of what could

happen, panic brought on by addictions, depressions from chemical imbalances, too many masters and too many commitments, and desires unfulfilled.

Many are anxious in their relationships, stressed by friction and diminished by betrayals. They suffer from all-too-real fears of legal actions, unfair competition, downsizing, and hostile takeovers.

Jesus himself advises us to be innocent and gentle as doves, but also wise as serpents. Beyond that, however, he reminds us – by way of a disarmingly simple question – that our lack of trust in him and in God is utterly useless: "Can any of you, by worrying, add a single hour to the span of your life?"

Sadly, the betrayals, the gossip, and the backbiting that are an inevitable part of every life keep many people from ever daring to trust. Clare Stober, a businesswoman who recently joined our community, writes:

> As an impediment to peace, mistrust is a biggie. We may try to defend ourselves and those we love by being wary, but we end up building walls of suspicion. If someone takes advantage of us or acts unfairly, we jump to assume the worst – and not just for that particular situation, but from then on. We see trust's cousin, vulnerability, as a sign of weakness, something stupid or simplistic.
>
> When we refuse to trust others, we may think we are protecting ourselves, but the opposite is true. Love is the greatest protection, the deepest security. When we are mistrustful, we can neither give nor receive love. We cut ourselves off from God and from each other.

At my community, as in any close-knit group of people, the proximity of our homes and the visibility of members' day-to-day lives creates a potential for unpeaceful ripples caused by speculation or gossip. Yet from the very start of

our community life, we have found that a mutual commitment to "open speaking" can maintain genuine trust and
peace.

There is no law but love. Love is joy in others. What, then,
is anger at them? Words of love convey the joy we have in
the presence of our brothers and sisters. It is out of the question to speak about another person in a spirit of irritation or
vexation. There must never be talk, either in open remarks
or by insinuation, against any brother or sister, or against
their individual characteristics—and under no circumstances
behind their backs. Gossiping in one's family is no exception.

Without this rule of silence there can be no loyalty and
thus no community. Direct address is the only way possible; it is the spontaneous brotherly or sisterly service we
owe anyone whose weaknesses cause a negative reaction in
us. An open word spoken directly to another person deepens
friendship and will not be resented. Only when two people
do not come to an agreement quickly is it necessary to draw
in a third person whom both of them trust. In this way they
can be led to a solution that unites them on the highest and
deepest levels.   *Eberhard Arnold, 1925*

Ellen Keiderling joined our community several decades ago
but still remembers her excitement on reading this piece for
the first time—and realizing that it was actually practiced:

When I first came to the community and discovered that
there would be no gossip—no talking about anyone behind
their back—it was like an enormous weight slipping off my
shoulders. Where I came from, gossip was a way of life. Like
anyone, I worried about what people thought and said of me
behind my back, but I hadn't really looked at those worries
closely and realized what an awful burden they were; how
much they can affect your life year after year. And now:
to know that if someone felt something wrong in me, they

would come and tell me – it was like new ground under my feet. I have failed in my commitment to direct speaking many times since then, but the trust has remained. It is something firm to return to and stand on.

All too often our peace of mind in relation to others is broken because we do not have this trust. For whatever reason, justifiable or not, we do not dare to believe that we will be loved just as we are, with all our weaknesses and foibles. But that is just what we must do. Rather than frittering away our lives in fear and mistrust, our attitude should be one of willingness to trust others time and again – even those who betray us.

Trust in God is every bit as vital. A writer once pictured a woman so consumed by her anxieties that when she goes to heaven, all that is left of her is a quivering little pile of worries. Humorous as the image may seem, it aptly describes the state of many people. If only they would realize that whether they trust him or not, God is there and has them in his hand! God knows the deepest secrets of our hearts and still loves us. He also knows everything we need before we ask him. For our part, we only have to come before him as we are – as children – and let him help us.

To some (mothers with babies or young children, for instance) such trust is not easy to come by. They are afraid of all the terrible things they read or hear in the news: wars and disasters, acts of terrorism and violent crime. Sometimes they may question the wisdom of bringing children into the world. It is not a new fear.

I was born during the bombing of Britain in World War II, and planes passed overhead every night. Twice bombs dropped nearby, once on our land and once in the next village. Even greater than my parents' fear of bombs, however, was their fear of a Nazi invasion. For them (as

German refugees who had spoken out against Hitler) and
for us children, this could have meant death, and it brought
my mother great anxiety whenever she thought about it.
Years later, remembering this period, my father wrote to a
couple he was counseling:

> Though we are not living in fear of bombers now, our time is
> one of great suffering and death. It is entirely possible that
> many of us—including parents of little children, like you—
> may one day have to suffer and die for our faith. I beg you
> from the depths of my heart to trust God completely. There
> are many frightening passages in the Bible, especially in the
> Revelation of John. But even there it says that God himself
> will wipe away the tears of all those who have suffered. We
> must really believe that Jesus came not to bring judgment but
> to bring salvation. "God so loved the world…" Hold on to
> this verse. It is a reminder of God's indescribable longing to
> save humankind. At the end we shall be one with God. We
> must believe this, for ourselves and for our children too.

Sometimes those who have most to fear, humanly speaking, are given the deepest sense of inward calm. A hospital
patient suffering from a terminal illness, a man on death
row, a dying accident victim—we may not expect such
people to be at peace. When death stares a person in the
face, however, superficial concerns that might distract
him in a less threatening situation fall to the side, and he
is forced to focus on the eternal. He is faced with a simple
choice: to beat his head against the wall, as it were, trying
to escape the inevitable, or to release himself into God's
hands in trust.

George Burleson, a close friend who battled cancer for
years, wrote to me:

> Since discovering that I have cancer and realizing how uncer-
> tain my future is, I have been learning how important it is

to trust completely and absolutely in the goodness of God. Only when I am able to do that does my anxiety disappear. Death comes to everyone – we are all in the same situation as regards dying – so to dwell on that certain event is a waste of time. Our lives are in God's hands. That is what matters, and to accept this brings peace.

Writer Dale Aukerman gives yet another testimony to the power of trust as an instrument of peace. Like George his peace is not rooted in a weak resignation to the fact that he may soon die; his love for life remains undiminished, and he will surely go down fighting. Yet his closeness to death does not unnerve him or unbalance him. His trust in a higher power gives him continual strength and an even keel.

On November 5, 1996, I found out that I had a tumor three and a half inches across on my left lung. Later tests showed that the cancer had spread to the liver, the right hip, and two spots in the spine. I learned that I could figure on living two to six months, with a median survival prospect of four months. It's amazing the reorientation of outlook that can come when you find out that you may have only a couple of months to live. Each day and each close relationship became more precious than before. Every morning I would think which day of the month it was – another day given to me by God. With fresh intentness I gazed at my family, my home, and God's creation, knowing that my time for seeing all this might very soon be at an end. In the anointing service held not long after the diagnosis, I confessed that I had not been giving God nearly enough attention. Through the cancer, God certainly gained much more of my attention.

When my sister Jane died of an especially lethal form of cancer at the age of fourteen, my mother saw this as God's will: God chose to take her, and who were we as human beings to challenge that? For some people this type of view gives comfort. I see such things somewhat differently. I don't

99

think God sends cancer or heart disease. When a drunken driver swerves into another car and kills a number of persons, I don't believe that is God's will. So much in the world is not what God intended and not what God wants...

But God is with us as one who stands against death. In more ways than we can notice or comprehend, God turns back the powers of death. As a boy I came near to being killed under a farm wagon. Several years later I almost died from what may have been arsenic poisoning. I've had close calls in automobiles...

After six cycles of chemotherapy, a regimen of nutritional supplements, and so much praying by a host of friends, I had another CAT scan, which showed that the tumor on my lung had shrunk to less than one-fourth of its earlier size. Two of the doctors spoke of that as a miracle. In an amazing way, and contrary to medical probabilities, God has held back death from me and given longer life.

In Ephesians 1:19–22 Paul writes of "the immeasurable greatness of God's power by which he raised Christ from the dead and made him sit at his right hand in the heavenly places." We read that God has put all things at the feet of Christ—that is, God has brought Christ to victorious dominion over all rebel powers. This is a biblical image for triumphant conquest and subjugating rule. The one who died and rose again is the victor over cancer, heart disease, AIDS, Alzheimer's, schizophrenia, abuse of children. He is victor over the exploitation of the poor, over the mindless blighting of God's good earth, over the madness of military spending and nuclear weapons.

But, we may ask, if Christ already has the victory over such things, why are they so much in evidence? Why do they seem to have such encompassing dominion? In a war there may be one decisive battle that determines which side will win. Because of that battle the one side is sure to go on to complete triumph, even though the other side still has troops in the field and the struggle continues. It's only a matter of time until that side is utterly vanquished.

Our hope does not have to do first of all with gaining eternal life after death. The towering hope given in the New Testament is that God's glorious kingdom will come, the invisible risen Lord will appear in splendor to recreate all that God has made, everything evil and destructive will be done away with. That is, history will turn out right. The human story will receive its God-given ending. God at some point will take total control of the stream of human events and bring in the unimaginable wonder of the new kingdom. Our hope is first a hope for the fulfillment of all that God has promised; and, quite secondarily, we hope to have our own tiny part in that.

Throughout my adult life I have been much involved in peace witness and peacemaking, and during these past months I've especially cherished verses about peace. There's one in John, where the risen Lord said to the fearful disciples in the upper room: "Peace be with you." Another one, which I thought of as I was being thrust in and out of an MRI tunnel, is from Philippians: "The peace of God, which passes all understanding, will keep your hearts and your minds in Christ Jesus."

Isaiah says, "Thou dost keep him in perfect peace, whose mind is stayed on thee, because he trusts in thee." This perfect peace, in the biblical understanding, is more than tranquility of spirit. It is wholeness of life and relationships that stands firm against all that tries to fragment and destroy us. It is a gift that can bear us up even when we walk through deep darkness.

Forgiveness

A rabbi asked his students: when, at dawn, can one tell the light from the darkness? One student replied: when I can tell a goat from a donkey. No, answered the rabbi. Another said: when I can tell a palm tree from a fig. No, answered the rabbi again. Well then, what is the answer? his students pressed him. Not until you look into the face of every man and every woman and see your brother and your sister, said the rabbi. Only then have you seen the light. All else is still darkness.   *Hasidic tale*

Human nature being what it is, the ability to see a brother or sister in every person we meet is a grace. Even our relationships with those who are closest to us are clouded now and then, if only by petty grievances. True peace with others requires effort. Sometimes it demands the readiness to yield; at other times, the willingness to be frank. Today we may need humility to remain silent; tomorrow, courage to confront or speak out. One thing remains constant, however: if we seek peace in our relationships, we must be willing to forgive over and over.

Each of us has been hurt at one time or another, and each of us has hurt others. And therefore, just as all of us must forgive, so all of us need to be forgiven. Without forgiveness, we will not find peace.

What is forgiveness? In my book *Why Forgive?*, which is devoted entirely to the subject, I pointed out that there is a forgiveness God offers, and the forgiveness that we grant each other as fellow human beings. The two are distinct, yet closely connected. In order to experience the peace God gives through his forgiveness, it seems we must first be willing to forgive others. To quote my father:

> God commands us to forgive others so that we ourselves can be forgiven, and this is important for all of our lives. Yet it is most important at the hour of our death. Those who are confident of having received forgiveness for their sins, and of having forgiven those who have hurt them, will be spared anguish in their final hours.

Forgiving has nothing to do with being fair, or with excusing wrongdoing; in fact, it may mean pardoning someone for something inexcusable. When we excuse someone, we brush his mistake aside. When we forgive someone, there may be good reason to hold onto our hurt, but we let go of it anyway. We refuse to seek revenge. Our forgiveness may not always be accepted, yet the act of reaching out our hand in reconciliation saves us from anger and indignation. Even if we remain wounded, a forgiving attitude will prevent us from lashing back at someone who has caused us pain. And it can strengthen our resolve to forgive again the next time we are hurt. Dorothy Day writes:

> God is on the side even of the unworthy, as we know from the story Jesus told of the prodigal son...Readers may claim that the prodigal son returned penitent to his father's house. But who knows, he might have gone out and squandered money on the next Saturday night, he might have refused to help with the farm work and asked to be sent to finish his education instead, thereby further incurring his brother's righteous wrath...Jesus has another answer to that one: to forgive one's brother seventy times seven. There are always answers, although they are not always calculated to soothe.

Ironically, those who suffer the worst things in life often forgive most readily. Bill Pelke, a Vietnam veteran from Indiana whom I met at an anti-death penalty event, lost his grandmother to a brutal murder, yet found closure in seeking reconciliation with the teenager who killed her.

Bill's grandmother was an outgoing woman who gave Bible lessons to children in her neighborhood. One afternoon in May 1985 she opened the door to four girls from the local high school several blocks away. Before she knew it, her attackers had knocked her to the floor. Minutes later, the house ransacked, they fled the premises in her old car, leaving her on the floor, bleeding to death from multiple stab wounds. Bill remembers:

> The girls were caught giving joy rides to friends in the stolen car. Later they went to trial. Sentencing came fifteen months later: one girl got thirty-five years, two got sixty years, and the last, Paula Cooper, got death. I was satisfied that at least one of them would be executed: I felt that if they weren't, the court would be saying my grandmother wasn't important, and I felt that she was a very important person.
>
> About four months after Paula was sentenced, I broke up with a girl I had been dating. I was trying to get the relationship back together and was very depressed. I couldn't find peace about anything.
>
> Then one day at work, while operating an overhead crane (I worked for Bethlehem Steel), I was thinking about why things hadn't worked out, also with my grandmother, and I just started praying. "Why, God? Why?" Suddenly I thought about Paula—this young girl, the youngest female in the country on death row—and I pictured her saying, "What have I done? What have I done?" I remembered the day Paula was sentenced to death; I recalled her grandfather in court, wailing, "They're killing my baby." He was escorted from the room. There were tears rolling down his cheeks...

I began to think of my grandmother, her faith, and what the Bible has to say about forgiveness. I recalled three verses: the one which says that for God to forgive you, you first need to forgive others; the one where Jesus tells Peter to forgive "seventy times seven"; the one where Jesus says, when he is being crucified, "Father, forgive them, for they don't know what they are doing." Paula didn't know what she was doing. When a girl stabs a woman thirty-three times, she is not in her right mind.

Suddenly I felt I had to forgive her. I prayed, right there and then, that God would give me love and compassion for her. That prayer changed my life. I no longer wanted her to die in the electric chair. What would an execution solve for me or anyone else?

When I had gone to the crane I was a defeated person: forty-five minutes later I emerged a completely different man.

Bill has visited Paula several times since her trial and sought to pass on his grandmother's faith to her—not by preaching, but simply by showing her compassion. He is no longer haunted by the image of his beloved grandmother lying butchered on the dining room floor—a room where the family had gathered for many of its happiest occasions. Naturally he still feels pain, yet this pain is mixed with a determination to make sure that other people are spared the agony of bitterness that he had to work through. "As long as I kept hating those girls, they continued to control my life. Once I chose to forgive them, I became free."

A committed activist in the growing "restorative justice movement," Bill now travels up and down the country with an organization called "Journey of Hope: from Violence to Healing." He is also a member of Murder Victims' Families for Reconciliation. "Forgiveness," he says, "is the only route from violence to healing. It spares you the corrosion of hatred and gives you freedom again to be at peace inside your own skin."

Most of us do not have to deal directly with murder; and many of the things we obsess over are even laughable by comparison. Still we may have a hard time forgiving. Especially if our resentment has grown over a long period, it will take time and effort to root out. And whether the hurt is real or imagined, it will eat away at us as long as we nurse it.

Not that we should swallow our hurts. To the contrary, people who push their grievances down into their subconscious in an attempt to forget them only cripple themselves. Before we can forgive a hurt, we must be able to name it. Sometimes it may not be possible (or helpful, even if it is possible) to confront the person we are struggling to forgive, and then the best solution is to share our pain with someone else we trust. Once we have done this, we must let go. Otherwise we may remain resentful forever, waiting for an apology that never comes. And we will remain separated from God.

> As long as we hold a grudge against someone, the door to God will be closed. It will be absolutely closed, with no way to him. I am sure that many prayers are not heard because the person praying has a grudge against someone, even if he or she is not aware of it. If we want God's peace in our hearts, we must first learn to forgive. *J. Heinrich Arnold*

Naturally we must seek to be forgiven too. After all, each of us is a sinner in God's eyes, even if our "goodness" prevents us from seeing ourselves in that light. A legend about Brother Angelo, a monk in Francis of Assisi's order, illustrates the problem beautifully.

On Christmas Eve, Brother Angelo cleans his simple mountain hut and decorates it for Mass. He says his prayers, sweeps the hearth, hangs a kettle over the fire, and then sits back to wait for Brother Francis, whom he expects later in the day. Just then three outlaws appear at the door, begging for food. Frightened and angry, Brother Angelo sends them away empty-handed, scolding and warning them that thieves are damned to hellfire.

When Francis arrives, he senses that something is not right. Brother Angelo then tells him about his visitors, and Francis sends him up into the mountains with a jug of wine and a loaf, to find them and ask their forgiveness. Brother Angelo is indignant. Unlike Francis, he cannot see the wild men as brothers—only as outlaws. He sets out obediently, however, and by nightfall (having followed the men's footsteps in the snow) he finds them and makes amends. Some time later, the legend goes, they leave their cave and join the order.

Gratitude

Live your life so that the fear of death can
never enter your heart. When you arise in the
morning, give thanks for the morning light.
Give thanks for your life and strength. Give
thanks for your food and for the joy of living.
And if perchance you see no reason for giving
thanks, rest assured the fault is in yourself.

Ascribed to Chief Tecumseh

The medieval mystic Meister Eckhart once suggested that
if the only prayer we ever said was "thank you," it would
still suffice. If we take his advice superficially, it might be
easy enough to follow. Yet to give thanks to God from the
bottom of our hearts for all he gives, and to live every day
in a spirit of gratefulness, is work for a lifetime.

What does it mean to be thankful? Henri Nouwen
writes:

> To be grateful for the good things that happen in our lives is
> easy, but to be grateful for all of our lives – the good as well
> as the bad, the moments of joy as well as the moments of
> sorrow, the successes as well as the failures, the rewards as
> well as the rejections – that requires hard spiritual work. Still,
> we are only truly grateful people when we can say thank-
> you to all that has brought us to the present moment. As long
> as we keep dividing our lives between events and people we
> would like to remember and those we would rather forget,
> we cannot claim the fullness of our beings as a gift of God to
> be grateful for.

Let us not be afraid to look at everything that has brought us to where we are now and trust that we will soon see in it the guiding hand of a loving God.

It is just as important to be thankful for the bad things that happen to us as for the good things. So long as we shrink from every predicament, every situation that frightens us or sets us on edge, we will never know peace. This does not mean we must silently accept everything that comes our way. Jesus himself says we should pray, "Lead us not into temptation." But because there is so much in life we cannot control, we must learn to look at things that test us not as obstacles, but as opportunities for growth.

French philosopher Simone Weil once wrote, "God continually showers the fullness of his grace on every being in the universe, but we consent to receive it to a greater or lesser extent. In purely spiritual matters, God grants all desires. Those who have less have asked for less." It is an intriguing thought.

Then again, if we truly mean the words, "Thy will be done," we will gratefully receive whatever God sees fit to give us. Even the children of Israel were answered with a rod of punishment at times. They did not only receive manna from heaven. As for the good things – family, food, house, friends, love, work – if we are honest, we must admit that we often take them for granted. We treat them as rights, rather than gifts.

Carroll King, a member of my church, notes that it is just when struggles or problems weigh most heavily on a person that gratitude can change his entire outlook on life:

> Once when I was in a deep depression, it came to me that if I looked for even just one thing to be thankful for, that would be the first step up. There is always something you can find to

be happy about…Freedom from fear and worry is something I have struggled with a lot in my life. But there is peace in laying your troubles in God's hands, and not only accepting the outcome he deems best for you, but being truly grateful for it—whatever it is.

The following lines from Jesuit priest Alfred Delp reflect the same attitude. They were written in 1944, from the prison where Delp awaited execution for speaking out against Hitler.

Outwardly things have never been worse. This is the first New Year I have ever approached without so much as a crust of bread to my name. I have absolutely nothing I can call my own. The only gesture of goodwill I have encountered is the jailers agreeing to fasten my handcuffs loosely enough for me to slip my left hand out. The handcuffs hang from my right wrist so I am able to write. But I have to keep one ear glued to the door—heaven help me if they should catch me at work!

Undeniably I find myself in the very shadow of the scaffold. Unless I can disprove the accusations on every point I shall most certainly hang.

Yet on the altar of my suffering much has been consumed by fire, and much has been melted and become pliable. It is one of God's blessings, and one of the signs of his indwelling grace, that I have been so wonderfully helped in keeping my vows. He will, I am confident, extend his blessing to my outward existence as soon as I am ready for the next task with which he wishes to entrust me. From this outward activity and intensified inner light, new passion will be born to give witness for the living God, for I have truly learned to know him in these days of trial and to feel his healing presence. The thought "God alone suffices" is literally and absolutely true.

Dietrich Bonhoeffer shows the same remarkable assurance in a prison letter he wrote to his fiancée, Maria Wedemeyer, on the eve of his execution: "You must not think that I am unhappy. What is happiness and unhappiness? It depends so little on the circumstances; it depends really only on what happens inside a person. I am grateful every day that I have you, and that makes me happy."

In my experience, the most common root of ungratefulness is not hardship, but a false understanding of happiness. Both Delp and Bonhoeffer say the presence or absence of hardship need not have anything to do with our state of mind or soul. "God alone suffices." If only that thought would arouse in us the endless gratitude that it should!

Nothing can satisfy us when selfish expectations make us discontented with our lot; hence the cliché, "The pasture is always greener on the other side of the fence." So long as our vision is limited by the blinders of our own wants and needs, we will not be able to see those of others, let alone the things we have to be grateful for. My father once wrote to an unhappy friend, "You will always find reasons to grumble. If you want to find peace, you must be willing to give them up. I beg you: stop concentrating on your desire to be loved. It is the opposite of Christianity."

William Marvin is an Anglican priest in Alabama I began corresponding with when he offered to help our church send humanitarian aid to Cuba. William has had more than his fair share (if there is such a thing) of suffering, but I have never heard him grumble. Despite one Job-like test after the next—a serious illness, the death of his youngest son, the loss of his job, and a divorce—he is still able to say, "Well, I've not yet suffered boils…" It is this attitude, I suspect, that is the key to his sense of peace.

I was dying. It was December of 1960. I was thirty-five years old. A few days earlier I had undergone surgery to remove a gangrenous appendix. Early in the morning a cloud of certainty that I was dying came over me, and with it, panic. I had a wife, three sons, and was in debt. I felt this would be the ultimate failure—to die, and leave them all destitute. Then a voice, clear and sharp, spoke in my ear: "So what! You're not even important to yourself! Only God!"

I have thought often about how God speaks to us. In my experience God usually speaks in a whisper, and uses few words. The event I touched on was the only time I recall him using a tone that was sharp, like a dash of cold water in the face. Recovery was very slow, but I did recover.

There have been other critical events in my life. My mother died suddenly when I was eight years old. A little over a year later my father married a woman much younger than he. Ours was not a happy home. My father was a school administrator, noted for strict enforcement of discipline and high academic standards. He carried this into the home. I wasn't mistreated physically, though my stepmother did slap me a time or two. Sarcasm and derision were the weapons of choice. The standing rule was, "What 'Mother' says, goes!" My teenage rebellion took the form of doing just enough in school to pass. This was the one area where I could defy them both, because it was so important to them. As soon as I graduated from high school I was told to leave. I lived with an uncle and aunt until I was old enough to be drafted into the army. My years in the service were intense. I saw battles, and saw men die. I was injured. After the army I went to college, though I had no clear sense of what to do with my life.

I married and soon had two sons, a house in the suburbs, a mortgage, and a car, and worked as a letter carrier. Three or four years later I became very discontented. Through much soul-searching and advice-seeking, I decided to become an Episcopal priest. After two months in seminary we went on a retreat. I was overwhelmed. I went to the retreat master, a monk from the Order of the Holy Cross, and told him that I had made a mistake: I was not worthy. His response was, "Of course you're not! None of us are. But we are what God has to work with."

After his graduation and ordination, William served in several parishes but soon realized that he had a different understanding of his position than his superiors did. Before long he was relieved of his duties. He found no new openings for a long time; after all, he had spoken out against the direction the Episcopal Church was taking. Finally he found a place in the Anglican parish where he now serves.

During those years, tragedy struck repeatedly. First William's youngest son was killed in a traffic accident; then his wife became involved with another man and moved out of the house, after which they divorced; his second son succumbed to alcohol and died at thirty-five of a massive stroke. There were some satisfactions, it is true: his eldest son became a successful attorney; his daughter earned a Ph.D. and joined the faculty of Notre Dame. William himself has found a family among the warm-hearted members of his parish. Yet his life has been anything but easy.

Have I found peace? I think so. I've fulfilled my obligations to my children; I am caring for the people of this parish, and I plan to do so as long as God wills.

I begin each morning reciting the *Venite* with its fourth verse, "In his hand are all the corners of the earth." At night I recite the *Nunc dimittis*, as well as the words Jesus spoke from the cross, "Father, into thy hands I commend my spirit." Throughout my waking hours the Jesus Prayer, a keystone of Eastern Orthodox mysticism, is often on my lips: "Lord Jesus Christ, Son of the Living God, have mercy on me, a sinner." Whenever I pray this, or one of my own thoughts, I realize anew that God's mercy is nothing less than his love. And I am warmed. I am grateful to know that I am forgiven, and accepted.

I have yet one thing I must do. I must die. Until then, even though I do plan ahead, I try to live each day as if it is my last.

It is not too much to believe that I have been in the hand of God from the day of my birth. My sons did not die, nor did my wife abandon her wedding vows, so that I would be tempered. These things happened because it is an imperfect world. Twenty-one years ago—after I had been fired from the church, my youngest son had been killed, my wife was recovering from a heart attack (and about to leave me), and I was working only ten hours a week—a friend suggested that I must feel as did Job. I said, "Well, I've not suffered boils." I've still not suffered boils.

Today I went, as I do every Friday, to the bedside of a man, a retired physician. He is dying. He has lost three daughters to cancer. His wife had cancer surgery a few years ago. Sundays I take Communion to him. He is not the only parishioner to have been given the special grace to bear burdens. Nearly everyone has at one time or another been visited by travail. I will cite one other, a young mother who suffered third-degree burns over forty percent of her body. Her husband abandoned her, and she is raising three fine young children alone. She is doing it very well. That God has permitted me to know people such as these, and to share my life with them, has been a great reward. It has brought me the peace of God, "which passeth understanding."

Honesty

You thought you were indifferent to praise for achievements which you would not yourself have counted to your credit, or that, if you should be tempted to feel flattered, you would always remember that the praise far exceeded what the events justified. You thought yourself indifferent – until you felt your jealousy flare up at someone else's naïve attempts to "make himself important," and your self-conceit stood exposed.

Concerning the hardness of the heart and its littleness, let me read with open eyes the book my days are writing – and learn.

Dag Hammarskjöld

If someone asked me to pick the most fundamental requirement for inner peace, I would probably take honesty. Whether taken to mean truthfulness in a general sense, or knowledge of one's condition, or the ability to call a spade a spade, or the willingness to admit failure in front of others, honesty is a basic premise for peace. We may strive and struggle for peace until our dying breath, but we will never find it as long as we are unwilling to place ourselves under the clear light of truth. Dishonesty is one of the greatest impediments along the path to peace, because it prevents us from finding a square footing on which to base our search.

As for conforming outwardly, and living your own life inwardly, I do not think much of that. When you get to God pulling one way, and the devil the other, each having his feet well braced – to say nothing of the conscience sawing transversely – almost any timber will give way.

Henry David Thoreau

The first step in turning to God, which is the same thing as turning toward peace, is recognizing our true condition. Before we can ever hope to find ourselves in God, we must admit that we are far from him. To do this, Thomas Merton says, we must "become conscious...that the person we think we are, here and now, is at best an impostor and a stranger. We must constantly question his motives and penetrate his disguises." Otherwise our attempts at self-knowledge are bound to fail.

Self-knowledge is only the first step. By itself it will not bring us peace, and may even lead us away from it by trapping us in a downward spiral of self-concern. My grandfather writes:

> Self-centeredness is a lying spirit. It is mortal disease. The self-centered person is deathly sick; he must be redeemed.
>
> Those who turn around themselves do not know that Christianity has an objective content, that it is actually a cause for which we can completely forget ourselves with our own little egos.
>
> Self-centeredness leads to a hypocritical attitude, to posing and to affected holiness. The people most endangered by it are the artificial saints who take such pains to be good. Their efforts are the root of their hypocrisy...
>
> To see God from your own point of view and make him relate to you is to view the world through a deceptive lens. I am not the truth, and because I am not the truth, I may not place my own person at the center of my thoughts. That would be making myself an idol. God must be in the center of my life.

We must realize that God's cause exists entirely outside of ourselves. It is not only that we are unimportant; we are dispensable. If we are honest we will admit that we are obstacles, adversaries of God. Not until we recognize this and see ourselves in this way can redemption begin.

To realize who we are means to face issues we have previously avoided, and to let ourselves be confronted. But it also means turning to God. Unfortunately, most of us do neither the first nor the second, let alone the third, because we fear that changes may be demanded of us. We are reluctant to give up the comfort of self-satisfaction. If only we recognized how much deeper and greater the peace is that comes from living with a fully awakened conscience!

Jeanette Warren, a member of our community, recently told me how, as a young woman, she looked for peace year after year—in labor movements and political organizations, campus groups and cooperatives and communities—but neglected the vital task of tending to the unpeace in herself first. Like countless others, she says her seeking bore fruit only once she was able to come to terms with the true state of her life by looking within, deeply and honestly.

Genuineness is as significant as self-knowledge in finding peace of mind. Without it we become hypocrites and must constantly adjust our image so as to manipulate the way others see us. In the Gospel of Matthew, Jesus specifically warns us against this. He says we must not try to appear devout in other people's eyes: "You hypocrites clean the outside of the cup and dish, but inside they are filthy, full of greed and self-indulgence. First clean the inside, and then the outside also will be clean." He goes even further: "You are like whitewashed tombs, which look beautiful on the outside but are full of dead men's bones and everything unclean. You appear righteous, but you are really full of hypocrisy and wickedness." Referring to these verses, my father writes:

> Let us never use religious words when we do not mean them. If we speak admiringly about discipleship, for instance, but resist its demands, it will harm our inner life. Let us be genuine and say what we think, even if we are off the mark, rather than use the right words without meaning them. Complete peace demands complete honesty. We cannot live in peace with our brothers unless we carry the truth in our hearts and are honest in our love.

Ungenuineness can become a habit. Once we are used to it, we may soon become downright deceitful as well. When this happens, it will take a concerted effort to strip away the falsehoods we have been hiding behind and to become honest again, both with ourselves and with those we have been deceiving. Zoroaster, the ancient prophet-poet of Persia, compares the situation to a battle:

> At the sight of this world
> I want to cry out:
> Can truth be really the better,
> when there is so much lying;
> and must I not join
> in their devilish howls?
>
> My God, do not forsake me;
> make me strong in this trial,
> and give me strength.
> Down, rebellious thought:
> the sword's at your throat!
>
> Only those who know
> the source at which life springs
> can draw from the eternal well.
> Only this refreshment
> is true comfort.

If Zoroaster seems excessive in portraying the agony of this struggle, it may be only because he is so eloquent. The battle between truth and deceit is not simply fought between two abstract opposites; it is a war between God and Satan, whom the Bible calls the "father of lies." Looking back at conversations I have had with people in times of crisis, I can say that this battle is always a hard one to fight, especially when someone has been deluded into believing that honesty is too high a price to pay for peace. Such a person may not even feel the need to fight things through at first, because he has blinded himself so completely to the fact that he has been living a lie.

In *The Brothers Karamazov*, Dostoevsky gives us just such a character: Fyodor Pavlovitch, an old man who mockingly asks Father Zossima what he must do to gain eternal life. The priest replies:

> You have known for a long time what you must do. Don't give way to drunkenness and incontinence of speech; don't give way to sensual lust and to the love of money. Above all, don't lie to yourself. The man who lies to himself and listens to his own lie comes to such a pass that he cannot distinguish the truth within or around him, and so loses all respect for himself and for others. Having no respect, he ceases to love, and in order to occupy and distract himself without love he gives way to passions and coarse pleasures, and sinks to bestiality in his vices, all from continually lying to other men and to himself. The man who lies to himself can be more easily offended than anyone. You know that nobody has insulted him, but that he has invented the insult for himself, has lied and exaggerated to make it picturesque, has caught at a word and made a mountain out of a molehill. He knows that himself, yet he will be the first to take offense, and will revel in his resentment till he feels great pleasure in it, and so pass on to genuine vindictiveness.

Shakespeare says much the same:

> This above all: To thine own self be true
> And it must follow, as the night the day,
> Thou canst not then be false to any man.

Human nature being what it is, this oft-quoted advice is easier to pass on than to practice. Even the most self-righteous person will not deny that he has lied before, and many times at that. As a matter of fact, most people yield to dishonesty already when they are small, and unless they are consistently and firmly educated to tell the truth, lying may become a habit that grows harder and harder to break. We might dismiss the childish act of snitching a cookie as normal, and it may be, but the same five-year-old who learns to "get by" doing that may have no qualms shoplifting, committing tax fraud, or cheating on his wife when he is an adult. As members of any church or synagogue will attest, religious people are just as prone to lying as their fellow human beings in the "secular" world.

If we are determined to find peace of heart, though, there is always a solution: to admit our wrongdoings to another person. As a specific rite or practice, confession is too complex an issue to address here. Simply admitting one's sins so as to find freedom and peace, however, need not be a complicated matter. Once we have recognized the disharmony between our true character, "warts and all," and the side of ourselves we present to others, we will remain painfully aware of the tension until we can reconcile the two. Even if we mend our ways and turn away from past wrongs, we cannot experience full peace of mind until we are willing to share our secret burdens with another person. That is why the Psalmist says, "I have no peace; there is sin in my bones."

To bare one's soul, even (or perhaps especially) to someone we love and trust, is always a painful exercise. But as we shall see later in this book, there is no way around it. If we want to find the peace of Christ, we must be ready to accept the anguish of his cross. We may never honestly desire this anguish, but if our yearning for God is deep enough, we will be willing to bear it and to let him renew us through it.

Accept me, my Lord; accept me for this while.
Let those orphaned days that passed without thee
    be forgotten.
Only spread this little moment wide across thy lap,
    holding it under thy light.
I have wandered in pursuit of voices that drew me
    yet led me nowhere.
Now let me sit in peace
    and listen to thy words
    in the soul of my silence.
Do not turn thy face from my heart's dark secrets,
    but light them till they burn away
    with thy love's fire.

Rabindranath Tagore

Peace can be lost in a moment—through stubbornness or deceit, pride, self-will, or the false comfort of an easy way out. Yet it is never too late to start looking for it again, even if it has eluded us for years. Whenever we are able to take an honest look at ourselves—who am I, not in the eyes of others, but in the sight of God?—it should not be hard to refocus on our need for Jesus. In his truth there is always peace.

Humility

Christ died to escape power, though men live to
wield it. Power is the greatest snare of all. How
terrible is power in all its manifestations – the
voice raised to command, the hand stretched
out to seize, the eyes burning with appetite.
Money had better be given away; organizations
had better be disbanded; bodies had better lie
separately. There is no peace at all, except in
looking across time at eternity beyond – as one
looks at a distant view from a mountain top.

Malcolm Muggeridge

Of all the stepping stones toward peace in this book,
humility may be the hardest to recognize. Humility is not
just gentleness or meekness. It demands vulnerability, the
willingness to be hurt. It is readiness to go unnoticed, to be
last, to receive the least. Humility offers nothing in the way
of peace as the world gives – and plenty that destroys it. Yet
it describes the way of Christ better than any other word. It
is the way of Christ. And as such it brings the deepest and
most lasting peace.

It is not coincidental that the angels' announcement of
Jesus' birth – "Glory to God in the highest, and on earth
peace, goodwill toward men" – was made first to shepherds.
For people with money, education, and culture, Christ's
message often seems too opposed to human wisdom to
accept. As John Cardinal O'Connor of New York has
written, "It is the opposite of everything the world teaches
about power and glory, about 'making it,' about wealth and
success and prestige."

Nor was it by chance that Jesus chose simple fishermen and not scribes to accompany him as he traveled and taught in Judea. Those who have fewer pretensions are more inclined to be open to the foolishness of the gospel and its peace.

There is plenty one could write about humility, but there is no substitute for simply practicing it from day to day. It is only through actually opening ourselves to others that we discover the hidden blessings of vulnerability, and only through accepting defeat that we learn to welcome the peace that self-surrender brings. That is why the apocryphal Book of Sirach says, "Accept whatever befalls you, and in times of humiliation be patient. For gold is tested in the fire, and those found acceptable, in the furnace of humiliation. Trust in him, and he will help you; make your ways straight, and hope in him."

As for how to become humble, there is also much that could be said. In his parable *The Shepherd*, the early Christian Hermas compares each human to a block of stone chosen by the Master Builder. If the block can be chiseled to fit a wall, it will be used. But if rough edges of arrogance and self-will make it too difficult to shape, it will be rejected. Jesus makes a similar comparison in his farewell words to his disciples: he speaks of the rigorous pruning each of us must undergo if we are to bear fruit: "I am the true vine, and my father the vinedresser. Every branch in me that does not bear fruit, he shall take away; and every branch that bears fruit he shall prune, that it may bear more fruit." Both parables are easy to comprehend. Whether we are humble enough to yield gracefully to the stonemason's blows or the gardener's knife is quite a different matter.

Tom and Monica Cornell, good friends in Marlboro, New York, and houseparents of the Catholic Worker farm there, say that in their experience, the peace of God – though freely bestowed – cannot be held onto without continual "pruning." Tom writes:

> It is hard to speak of one's own prunings, of the way God has cut one down to size. Jesus spoke of a landowner who inspected a fig tree that had borne no fruit for three years. He was about to have it cut down when his gardener convinced him otherwise. "Sir, leave it for this year also, and I will dig around it and dung it. Then it may bear fruit. If not, cut it down" (Luke 13:6–9). That's what God does with us. To make us produce, he digs around and prunes us, too, and sometimes the dung is piled deep.
>
> "Why me, Lord?" I have heard people cry when some hard blow falls, and I have heard myself say it too. "Why me, Lord?" Saint Teresa of Avila, the great reformer of the Carmelite Order, was once fording a river on horseback. Her horse stumbled and threw her into the water. She complained to God. "This is how I treat my friends," came a voice. "No wonder you have so few of them!" Teresa answered.
>
> I lost my father when I was fourteen years old. It was not a sudden blow, ten years in coming. My father ruined his health early working to support his family and took ten years to die. I knew when he left for the sanitarium the day after his fifty-second birthday that I would not see him alive again. Six months later my mother split the earth with her grief, and a chill of terror gripped me. This couldn't be happening. How would we live?
>
> It is strange to think, stranger to say, that it was all for the better. "All things work together for good for those that love God" (Rom. 8:28). Even this?
>
> I can imagine that, had my father lived as I grew to maturity and took the rebel path of Christian discipleship, we would have been locked in terrible combat. He was an extreme national chauvinist. My mother would have been in the middle. As it happened, my oedipal struggle was with his ghost, and it never ends.

We lived, my mother, my sister, and I, and by working lots and spending little, I was able to make it through a Jesuit preparatory school and college, Fairfield. At work, as a teen-ager in a factory, I learned valuable lessons by experience. The work I did was repetitive, an operation performed in a crouched position, not standing and not sitting. It involved both hands and one foot in an act that took about two seconds and was performed for sixty hours a week, ever faster, piece-work. I never saw the finished product of my labor, nor did I ever feel that what I was doing made any sense.

Life was good after I found my vocation at the Catholic Worker. On reading *The Long Loneliness* by Dorothy Day, everything fell into place, faith and experience. I was integrated into the intellectual core of the Worker even before graduating from college; there were few enough of us. After graduation I came to New York City and went out on assign-ment, as it were, for the Catholic Worker, first to an agri-cultural resettlement project in the South, then to projects of the larger peace movement, working with A. J. Muste and his associates in the Committee for Nonviolent Action and the War Resisters League, a roster of all the big names of the radical nonviolent movement of the period. I wanted to learn about practical nonviolence, and I wanted to get to know the leaders personally so that I could bring this knowledge and those contacts back to the Catholic Worker. I wanted to be an ambassador to the larger movement, and I was received as such.

Before long I was seen to be something of an authority on war and peace and nonviolence, though on what basis has never been clear. But I sensed that God's will for me was to help develop the theory and the practice of nonviolence within the Catholic Worker movement. The work was highly successful and personally very satisfying.

The most severe pruning is to see one's life work undone. That is what, it seemed to me, was happening halfway through. I found myself in a darkening wood. The nonviolent movement was running down. Even before his murder, black nationalists and separatists had overshadowed Martin Luther King; their slogan: by any means necessary. Major elements in the anti-war circles had compromised their pacifism for a "revolutionary imperative." Activists appropriated the term nonviolence, but without any reference to Gandhian principles or practice. And I was fired from my job after fifteen years.

It was a good job. The Fellowship of Reconciliation is the largest ecumenical and interreligious pacifist organization in the world. It paid me enough to raise my family and to extend hospitality (essential for a Catholic Worker), to keep a modest home and a used car, and it gave me access to a large stage. I traveled the country, Latin America, the Middle East, and Europe, speaking and writing on nonviolence and strengthening the network of nonviolent activists. I looked forward to a pension that would eventually enable me to work independently, on my own schedule, and I foresaw an ever-widening arena of operations. Then it all came crashing down. My job was "eliminated."

Then came three years working freelance, doing as valuable work as ever (if not more), but I could not make a living. We lost our house. That broke my heart.

Leaving the FOR caused me great pain. It was a pruning. Ironically, the most important and lasting work I did for peace came after the separation, during my years in the wilderness. At my urging the Catholic Church in the United States pledged itself to the support of any who were troubled by the military draft, and I was allowed, with the bishops' approbation and advertisement, to bring a draft counselor training program to several dioceses throughout the country. At the same time, Archbishop Oscar Romero, as president of the Central American bishops' conference, gave me an assignment to gather support for peace in El Salvador. He and two American nuns, participants in the program I organized, watered the Lord's field with their blood shortly after. But I still could not support my family.

It is said that if God closes one door, he opens another. But not necessarily right away. In desperation I took a job teaching eighth grade in a public junior high school in New Hampshire, "my northern exile," for one year. This was a bewildering pruning. I could make no sense of it at all. In late winter a telephone call came in, from the U.S. Catholic Conference, the action arm of American bishops. "The Church needs you," said Ed Dougherty, in mild humor. He asked if I would please accept an invitation to meet with five bishops who were drafting a peace pastoral to be published in 1983. There were scads of consultants invited from the Pentagon and the State Department to consult with the drafting committee, but only three pacifists. Could I make it? The heavens opened for a moment.

Then the Waterbury (Connecticut) Area Council of Churches called me and my family to help in a soup kitchen. What bliss, to exchange some one hundred hormone-crazed eighth graders for three hundred alcoholics, drug addicts, arsonists, burglars, thieves, and murderers, and a larger number whose crime was simply that they were very poor! I was giving them something they wanted – soup and a smile – and they let me into their lives. Had I not been pruned of my respectable job I might have become a "peace bureaucrat," but my burglars kept me honest.

Now my wife Monica and I have been called back to the "mother community" of the Catholic Worker movement, and I am able again to write and to speak and to travel, a man diminished, in the sense of being pruned of delusion. How naïve and presumptuous I was ever to think that in my lifetime I would see, through my efforts, an extension of Gandhi's work in India here in America! During the Cold War I had access to the best minds in peace and radical movements on four continents. We plotted the course that events would take. And we were wrong about almost everything! More than that, the movement I had thought I was to serve and help develop, the Gandhian movement of nonviolence, was sidetracked—derailed by fools and, yes, let it be said, scoundrels. This caused me resentment and anger that lasted many years. But I had to ask myself if I was not "putting myself in charge." "Let go and let God," they say in recovery programs for addicts. Here come the pruning shears again.

When I was young I wanted to do grand things. Then I met Dorothy Day, and the first time I heard her speak it was to the effect: think not on the morrow; cast caution to the winds. She said, "There are great things to be done, and who will do them but the young. Yet how will they do them if all they think about is their own security?" Dorothy was younger when she said that than I am now. I might temper her advice, as she might, too, with greater experience. But it remains that we did do great things, by accident, or by the grace of God.

We took part in the dismantling of the legal structures of racial segregation in the U.S. through nonviolence (though today, forty years later, the condition of the poorest blacks is worse than it was then). We reintroduced nonviolence into Catholic and mainline Protestant consciousness (though the threat of war remains, and it is more grave in many ways). Now a new generation thirsts for the heroic. "There are great things to be done...Dare to struggle!"

In struggle I learned that the grandest thing is simply to do the ordinary things with ordinary people in the spirit of love, to enter the lives of the poor, to love them and to allow oneself to be loved by them, and to be guided by the needs of the community and obedient to its voice. St. Thérèse of Lisieux called it "the little way." This is what brings true peace, the peace of Christ. It is a fruit of the Holy Spirit, and it grows upon the pruned vine.

Tom's words contain plenty to chew on regarding humility and peace. So do the following thoughts from Derek Wardle, an Englishman who stumbled across our community during World War II and soon decided to stay.

Derek grew up in a comfortable middle-class home but became aware of poverty when he took a train through London's East End. Films like *The Stars Look Down* (about Welsh coal miners) and *The Grapes of Wrath* also opened his eyes and brought about the first stirrings of conscience. Later he marched in May Day parades, attended rallies, joined the Left Book Club, and became a Communist.

Like many Europeans of his day, Derek says he was blind to the evils of Stalinism. He regarded the Soviet Union as a socialist utopia. And, as is the case with so many young people, his political leanings were a source of narrow-mindedness. "I classified people according to their affiliations and was highly disrespectful and sometimes hateful toward those I disagreed with." Only later did he see that his arrogance was as much a seed of violence as the bourgeois class consciousness he had been protesting in the streets.

In August 1939, just a month before the outbreak of the war, I went to Leipzig to visit my pen pal, a convinced member of the Hitler Youth, and learned the lesson that "even" Nazis were people. Although I was called home after three days by anxious parents, the experience was enough to shatter my habit of categorizing people as "good" and "bad" guys, and to make me get to know them as people. This lesson has stayed with me...

I have learned how vital it is to give up self in all its forms—from excessive concern with one's weakness and failures, to outright pride and ambition. Whenever I have given way to any of these things I cannot know peace; when I am humbly and fully surrendered to God, it is given. It is always a choice, and the same choice stands before every young person today, though they may have to learn things the hard way, as I did.

Mother Teresa says that self-knowledge brings one to one's knees. That has certainly been the case with me. I no longer believe *I* can change the world; I believe God must. I will still go on protesting injustice – racism, capitalism, nationalism, whatever. Yet I feel it is the daily little acts of love that prove our sincerity just as much as the bigger things we do.

It is easy to become frustrated by the power of evil in the world, and to become embittered. But we can also be humble and look for ways to turn our indignation into something positive, such as service to others.

Obedience

He comes to us as one unknown – without a name – as of old, by the lakeside, he came to those who knew him not. He speaks to us the same word – "Follow thou me!" – and sets us to the tasks he wants us to fulfill. He commands, and to those who obey him, whether they be wise or simple, he will reveal himself in the toils, the conflicts, the sufferings which they shall pass through in his fellowship – and, as an ineffable mystery, they shall learn in their own experience who he is.   *Albert Schweitzer*

Though for a pastor my father was unusually reserved in his use of religious language, he never hesitated to remind us children of an important truth by using the Bible to illustrate it. Whenever Papa spoke about compassion, the story of Jesus and the woman at the well seemed to leap to mind; when he was talking about conviction, he would quote John's words in Revelation about God spitting out of his mouth those who are lukewarm. To illustrate the importance of obedience, he used the passage where Jesus sends his disciples to fetch a colt.

> When Jesus asked those two men to go and get him a colt, they had no other task in the whole world more important than fetching it. Someone might have said to them, "You are called to greater things; anyone can go find a donkey!" Yet there was nothing greater for them at that moment than fetching the donkey for Christ. For myself and for each

individual, I wish that we might do every task God calls us to do, great or small, with such readiness. There is nothing greater than obedience to Christ.   *J. Heinrich Arnold*

For most of us, obedience is a sticking point. We call ourselves disciples, but we lack the joy and submission that should be part and parcel of bearing that name. Even when the task in front of us is straightforward, pride may keep us from doing it, and because of this we get nowhere in our search for peace.

Given our society's worship of the individual and individualism, this is hardly surprising. From childhood on we are taught, and we teach our children, that it is important to follow our instincts, to show initiative, to develop our leadership skills. All this is good and proper. But what about the other side of the coin – the equal worth of knowing how to follow? When will we learn that our own best interests are not necessarily those of God, and that our insistence on being our own boss and doing our own thing may bear more bad fruits than good ones?

Sadly, people who submit to others when there are no tangible benefits (or when there are sacrifices involved) are often seen as spineless, if not brainwashed. Authority, including divine authority, is despised. The very idea of honoring father and mother is scorned as old-fashioned; respect for the elderly is a thing of the past; and God is often the object of crude ridicule.

We have forgotten the disobedience of the children of Israel and the wrath of God that followed it time and again. We have forgotten that the peace we seek comes from a Creator who brought order out of chaos. God brings life where there was only "waste and void." He is not a God of disorder, but of peace.

The road from self-determination to freewilling submission is not an easy one. Even for Jesus, the hardest battle was to obey. During his last long night in the Garden of Gethsemane he sweated blood as he struggled to submit: "Let this cup pass me by." But later he was able to say, "Not my will, Father, but thine."

Obedience, it has been said, is the root of grace, but that does not make it any more palatable. Dorothy Day felt the call to discipleship early in life (though only vaguely), but she first threw herself into other, "more important" things. There was the lure of liberal arts, and then politics; then there was travel and a taste of the Roaring Twenties in New York City, Italy, and Hollywood. There was also a novel, several film scripts, an abortion, a short-lived marriage, and a baby daughter. Still it did not dawn on her that she was running from God, and that her yearning would never be stilled until she was obedient to him.

Then came an unforgettable night in a Greenwich Village bar where a friend, playwright Eugene O'Neill, recited Francis Thompson's "Hound of Heaven" for her – a poem whose message left her reeling. It contains the verse:

> I fled Him, down the nights and down the days;
> I fled Him, down the arches of the years;
> I fled Him, down the labyrinthine ways
> Of my own mind; and in the mist of tears
> I hid from Him, and under running laughter.

Dorothy experienced what can only be called a conversion. Leftist friends mocked her new interest in the Gospels: didn't she of all people, a radical socialist, know that religion was just a crutch for the weak? But Dorothy dug in her heels. Jesus promised the new society of peace and justice they were all looking for, she said; and if the Christians they knew were soft-minded hypocrites, that was not Jesus' fault. She was determined to give him a try.

By the time Dorothy passed away in 1980, it was clear she had done more than try. Shaken by the hopelessness of the unemployed millions during the Depression years, she dropped all ambition of becoming a famous writer and spent the rest of her life serving God and the poor, in whose face she saw Jesus. Whether publicizing her views on non-violence with acts of civil disobedience (she was imprisoned many times), or "spreading the Word" through her books and newspaper articles, she was passionate in her belief that Christ demanded more than words.

As far as Dorothy could tell, he demanded "works of mercy:" feeding the hungry, housing the homeless, visiting the sick, and cleaning up after hundreds of noisy, often ungrateful guests in her soup line, day after day, year after year. This she did gladly at the Catholic Worker, a communal hospitality house she founded on New York's gritty Lower East Side.

Often our reasons for disobedience sound sensible enough: we lack courage, or strength, or clarity of vision; we feel we are not suited to the task ahead of us. Just as often, the real reasons are less noble: laziness, pride, obstinacy, and self-will. Mother Teresa, speaking from years of experience with her fellow Missionaries of Charity, tackled the root of this problem—our desire to understand just why we should do something we have been asked to do, and the temptation, once we know, to do it our own way.

> It is true that your work may be better carried out if you know how God wants you to carry it out, but you will have no way of knowing that, other than by obedience. Submit to your superiors, just like ivy. Ivy cannot live if it does not hold fast to something; you will not grow or live in holiness unless

you hold fast to obedience. Be faithful in small things, then. It is in steadfastness and obedience that true strength lies.

Like new members of many religious communities, including my own, novices in Mother Teresa's order take a vow of obedience when they join. To live out such a vow is a lifelong task, however, as Thomas Merton once noted in a letter to a young friend:

> You are probably striving to build yourself an identity in your work, out of your work and your witness. You are using it, so to speak, to protect yourself against nothingness, annihilation. That is not the right use of your work. All the good that you will do will come not from you but from the fact that you have allowed yourself, in the obedience of faith, to be used for God's love. Think of this more, and gradually you will be free from the need to prove yourself, and you can be more open to the power that will work through you without your knowing it.
>
> The great thing after all is to live, not to pour out your life in the service of a myth; and we turn the best things into myths. If you can get free from the domination of causes and just serve Christ's truth, you will be able to do more and will be less crushed by the inevitable disappointments. Because I see nothing whatever in sight but much disappointment, frustration, and confusion.
>
> Our real hope, then, is not in something we think we can do, but in God who is making something good out of it in some way we cannot see. If we can do his will, we will be helping in this process. But we will not necessarily know all about it beforehand.

A story in the Second Book of Kings makes the same point in a memorable way. When Naaman, a royal servant, goes to Elisha and asks him to heal his leprosy, the prophet tells him to go and wash in the Jordan River seven times.

Naaman, feeling he has been ridiculed, stalks off in a rage. Later his servants try to reason with him: "If the prophet had told you to do some great thing, wouldn't you have done it? Then you should also obey him now." Finally Naaman is persuaded; though still angry and embarrassed, he goes down to the Jordan and obediently lowers himself in the water seven times. At this, we read, "his flesh became as healthy as a little child's, and he was healed."

Daniel Berrigan has noted how in the Bible generally, the greatest acts of faith were done without respect to outcome or success. Abraham took up his son and went into the mountains, because God had told him to. Gabriel came with the most unbelievable news, and Mary simply believed and obeyed.

Jumping to the twentieth century, the letters of Ewald von Kleist, a victim of Nazi persecution, bear witness to the same readiness and obedience. To quote from one of them:

> Seek your peace in God and you will find it. He holds us by the hand and leads us and finally receives us in glory. And obey his will; he will take care of everything.
>
> Never, absolutely never, not even in the most secret chamber of your heart, rebel against what God has inflicted upon you, and you will see how incomparably easier it will be to bear anything. I have not written a single word that does not stand for something I have experienced myself, with gratitude to God. It is true for all eternity. All this does not simply fall into one's lap. It must be fought for in a constant struggle with oneself, a daily and sometimes even hourly struggle. But the inward sense of blessedness, which compensates for everything, will not escape you. Believe me: I have experienced it.

A cynic might say Kleist was able to see things with such clarity because he had no choice, and in a way this might be true. To someone who stands before death's door, the important things of life stand out in stark relief. Yet Kleist's attitude – "never, never rebel" – is doubly challenging when one considers the circumstances. Given his impending execution, this attitude would have no bearing whatsoever on his fate. Obedience could not save him.

Those of us whose trials consist merely of too many choices are usually far more self-serving and willful. Convenience, not obedience, drives many of our decisions. We may not run from a recognized task or calling, but we will look for an "out" and seek the solution everywhere except where God has an answer waiting. Like the ancient Israelites, we prefer to follow our own plans, and God is left to sigh at our stupidity.

> The commandment I give to you today is not hidden from you and is not far away. It is not in heaven, so that you say, "Who will go up to heaven and bring it down for us, so that we can hear it and do it?" Nor is it beyond the sea, so that you say, "Who will cross the sea and bring it back to us, so we can hear it and do it?" But the teaching is very near you; it is in your mouth and in your heart, so that you can do it.
>
> *Deuteronomy 30*

Decisiveness

Unless a definite step is demanded, the call
vanishes into thin air, and if people imagine
they can follow Jesus without taking this step,
they are deluding themselves like fanatics.
Although Peter cannot achieve his own conversion, he can leave his nets.

Dietrich Bonhoeffer

In speaking with the men and women whose insights are
incorporated in this book, a common thread stands out: the
role of choice and free will in their search for peace. Peace
may be a gift, but it is also a "pearl of great price." And the
act of setting out to find it and sell all one has for it must be
preceded, in every case, by a decision.

Viktor Frankl has written that peace means freedom in
the face of three things: our instincts or "lower nature,"
our inherited traits or disposition, and our surroundings.

> Certainly man has instincts, but these instincts must not have
> him. As for inheritance, research on heredity has shown how
> high is the degree of human freedom in the face of predispo-
> sition. As for environment, we know that it does not make
> man, but that everything depends on what man makes of it,
> on his attitude toward it.
>
> Thus, man is by no means merely a product of heredity
> and environment. There is another element: decision. Man
> ultimately decides for himself! And, in the end, education
> must be education toward the ability to decide.

Few of us, Frankl goes on, make important life choices
with any degree of decisiveness. Backtracking here and

compromising there, we often lack the backbone to stand by our own decisions. Because of this we remain in a continual state of angst. At times we hold a planless, day-to-day attitude toward whatever comes our way. At others we are fatalistic, defeatist. One day we exhibit spinelessness and have no clearly defined opinion at all; the next we cling so strongly and stubbornly to an idea we become fanatical. Ultimately, Frankl says, all these symptoms can be traced back to our fear of responsibility, and the indecision which is its fruit.

Naturally some choices we face are easy to make, while others can be made only with the most agonized soul-searching. Even then, God can guide us to make the right move if we are open to his leading. I am not speaking here of thunderbolts or flashes (most of us, it seems, receive very few answers without praying for them), but of "hours of grace" – times when God comes close to us, softens our hearts, and opens our inner ear to him.

Such "hours" may come to us once, twice, or even several times. If we are open to them, God's voice may speak so clearly that the right path forward will become obvious; we only have to follow it. Alfred Delp writes:

> There are times in each of our lives when we are filled with self-disgust, when consciousness of our failure tears the mask from our self-assurance and self-justification, and reality stands revealed – even if only for an instant. Such moments of truth can produce a permanent change. Yet our natural tendency is to avoid them. This is because our pride and cowardice (and our realization that the only way out of the situation is to humble ourselves and submit to God) tempt us to declare the moment unreal and counterfeit.
>
> The awakening shock may only come when our sin has gone so far that it finally saps our self-confidence and forces us to take a closer look at ourselves. Everything depends

on whether we take this loss of self-confidence (which is really a loss of pride) seriously, or whether we pass it off as "weakness."

To try to recover speedily from such moments means to sink even further into our sin and error. Things will only get worse. We will become "immunized" to our sin, and we will no longer be able to distinguish the false from the true. Often we will even end up defending our error with pious clichés like "self-determination," the "right to choose," and so on.

In 1997, John Winter, an elderly member of my church, wrote to me that the most fruitful chapters of his life were those he entered with a firm decision – and the intention of sticking to it, come what may.

I left school at sixteen and started working in the lab of a firm that made lead pipe and paint, and went up to London to study for a science degree in the evenings. That was a rough time: work during the day; a train ride, classes, and another train ride each evening (getting home about eleven o'clock); and homework on the weekends. When I was nineteen I had to register for military service. I was a pacifist, so I had decided to register as a conscientious objector. When I told my boss, he pointed out that the firm was now making bullets instead of pipes and paint, and that my stand wouldn't quite go together with the company's. I was in shock, and can still remember that weekend as if it were today – the hours spent trying to discern what I should do. I couldn't honestly carry on with my job, but to leave it seemed unthinkable too.

A pacifist friend of mine was going through similar tensions at this time. Later, however, finding no solid basis on which to stake his refusal to take part in the war, he changed his mind and joined the Royal Air Force.

That weekend – when I had to choose whether I was going to be true to what I believed about war, and act on it, or go on with life as usual – was decisive for me. It cost me many sleepless hours, but finally I knew what I had to do: give up my job.

It seems a very small thing now, but it was very big for me then. Perhaps it was the first time I really had to choose between my own wishes and what my conscience was telling me to do. I can only say now, fifty-eight years later, that at that moment I experienced something of the peace given by God. I have had to think of it several times since then in my life, when my conscience has prodded me to take a step I didn't want to take at first. Each time I followed my conscience, it has led to an inner peace, which is absolutely true and cannot be described.

On the other side of the coin, life has also made me realize that if you hear a call but don't follow, it does something to you inside, and maybe the next time God speaks you will not be able to hear him as clearly. God may not just give up on us when we are proud and stubborn, but I feel sure there comes a point when it is too late.

After I left my job I was unemployed for months and months. I looked for work that was not connected with the war, but there was none, at least not in what I was trained for, and to be idle is a terrible thing. I couldn't even find work in an office or shop. Yet I cannot deny that even then I was at peace about what I had done, and felt my life was in God's hands.

All of us know people who (unlike John) cannot find peace within themselves because they cannot stick to a decision. Such people go through life like a sailboat without a keel, tipping at the slightest gusts and reaching the goals they set out to meet only with the greatest trouble. Some never make it at all, but spend year after year trying to decide what to throw themselves into next. In the worst cases I know of, such indecision leads to emotional imbalance and even complete mental instability.

In matters of faith, decisiveness is essential for a healthy, productive life. Jesus offers unending peace, but first he demands our promise of unending loyalty. Perhaps the reason many people do not experience the one is their unwillingness to be confronted by the other. I have always loved the words, "Unless you eat the flesh of the Son of Man and drink his blood, you have no life in you." That is not a philosophy to be pondered or probed or analyzed. It is a rash claim, and we must choose either to reject it or to embrace it. No one can be indifferent to Jesus. We must decide for him or against him.

Bart (not his real name) is a young man from my community. Almost twenty-one, he was near the top of his class at a prestigious East Coast university and looking forward to graduation. He had already received several good job offers. Yet Bart was not entirely happy: deep down, he was beginning to see the emptiness of life in the fast lane, and gradually the thought came to him that he should drop everything and return to the community he grew up in, even though this would mean submitting his talents, time, and money to a common cause, and working wherever he was needed. In the middle of his last semester, Bart quit school and wrote the following letter, which he has allowed me to quote:

> I've been really torn apart these past two days. In a way, I have felt a tremendous pull to stay in school, finish my degree, get a job and do some work for an admirable cause like public radio. But I also feel called to serve at home, in the community. I've tried to rationalize staying here and doing my own thing, splitting away from the community, or whatever. But finally I've realized that just won't cut it.
>
> I read in Matthew last night about the disciples dropping their nets and running after Christ. That's what I have to do

now: get the hell out of this place, which has given me lots of theoretical knowledge and plenty of practical skills, but not much else, at least not in the way of personal or spiritual growth...

Sometimes you have to make decisions without knowing quite why or understanding what you're doing. I definitely don't understand all of the reasons why I've decided to do this, but then again none of us really understands much of what we are doing. I've got to trust in God more. I think he's trying to tell me something right now, and I hope I can listen to it.

If such a decision seems crazy, it is only because it flies in the face of convention. It runs against the widespread idea that even if we hear a clear call from God, it is still prudent to stop and consider it—as the cliché goes, to "pray about it." But didn't Jesus tell his disciples simply to drop their nets and follow him? And doesn't he advise us to let the dead bury their dead? Perhaps we are overly sure that he will give us time to weigh our options. Let us ask God to help us see the course our lives are taking with the eyes of faith. Then everything will assume its proper proportion.

The question of where to live and what to do is really insignificant compared to the question of how to keep the eyes of my heart focused on God. I can be teaching at Yale, working in the bakery at the Genesee Abbey, or walking around with poor children in Peru, and feel totally useless, miserable, and depressed in all these situations.

There is no such thing as the right place, the right job, the right calling or ministry. I can be happy or unhappy in all situations. I am sure of it, because I have been. I have felt distraught and joyful in situations of abundance as well as poverty, in situations of popularity and anonymity, in situations of success and failure. The difference was never based on the situation itself, but always on my state of mind and heart.

When I knew I was walking with God, I always felt happy and at peace. When I was entangled in my own complaints and emotional needs, I always felt restless and divided.

It is a simple truth that comes to me now, in a time when I have to decide about my future. Deciding to do this, that, or the other for the next five, ten, or twenty years is no great decision. Turning fully, unconditionally, and without fear to God is. Yet this awareness sets me free.

Henri J. M. Nouwen

Repentance

Fallen man is not simply an imperfect creature who needs improvement: he is a rebel who must lay down his arms. Laying down your arms, surrendering, saying you are sorry, realizing that you have been on the wrong track and getting ready to start life over again from the ground floor – that is the only way out of a hole. This process of surrender, this movement full speed astern, is what Christians call repentance.

C. S. Lewis

"Repent, for the kingdom of heaven is at hand!" may be one of the Bible's most familiar verses, yet for generations Christians have avoided its impact as zealously as they have repeated it. It is one thing to be humble, gentle, or kind. But remorseful? To admit one's wrongs and weep for them? To repent? Harsh as it may seem, there is no peace without repentance. Just as Christ's suffering on the cross remains meaningless for us as long as we refuse to suffer with him, so his resurrection holds promise for us only if we are willing to go with him to the grave. There is no new life without death.

Repentance means death to the old self, the old Adam. It means turning away from the corruption of a fallen world, and placing oneself willingly and gladly under the light of God, who sees the deepest secrets of our hearts. When a person repents, a heart of stone becomes a heart of flesh, and every thought, every emotion is transformed. A person's entire outlook changes.

As a counselor, I have noticed that one of the most wide-spread causes of emotional turmoil is immorality. I am not saying that lust is worse than other sins. The apostle Paul makes it clear that pride and self-righteousness, for instance, are just as opposed to God. In fact, they may be even harder to overcome than other sins, since they are not as obvious. But because our sexuality is our best-guarded, most intimate sphere, secret sexual sins are often the most burdensome.

Years ago, a young woman came to our community. Sue (not her real name) grew up in an educated family and had everything she wanted materially. But she was miserable. She longed for wholeness and peace in her life, yet she was so weighed down by self-hatred and guilt, so careworn, she felt at the end of her rope.

If someone had asked me, in 1972, what "peace" meant, I would have told them, "an end to the war in Vietnam." Growing up in the sixties, I had no idea peace was anything deeper than that.

As one of four children of an often violent, alcoholic father, I was part of a typical dysfunctional family – very middle class, very unhappy. At the age of nine or ten I began toying with sex. I noticed that if a boy in my neighborhood "wanted" me I had power over him, and I began to use my looks to the fullest. I led many boys and men on in this way without ever intending to have sex with them. I just wanted to control them. Little did I know that evil chains were binding me link by link.

In 1968, at the age of fourteen, I found my sister and her husband dead in their apartment. Married for only three months to a Navy man, this beautiful twenty-two-year-old woman's life was over. Was it a quarrel? Had he had a breakdown? Was it the fact that he was possibly headed for

Vietnam? Only two dead bodies and a gun were left to tell the tale when my other sister and I walked in their door...

Sue's life was thrown into utter confusion after this. Having experimented with Ouija boards and mock séances, she was filled with a deep fear of the supernatural world and felt haunted by the presence of her sister's soul. But she was unable to tell anyone her fears.

Full of anger and hatred, especially toward my father, I began to lose myself in amphetamines, hashish, and marijuana while getting drunk each weekend with a different man. By the time I was seventeen I had done just about everything, sexually... Ironically, some friends and I were part of the whole peace, love, anti-war thing that was so strong in those days. True, there was a great deal of idealism in the early 1970s, but the selfishness in many sex-lives was the opposite of the ideal.

When I was nineteen I arrived at the intentional community where I am a member today. I was a haunted, burdened, desperate woman, and the evil of my past weighed so heavily on my soul that it took away any appearance of youth. People were sure I was at least in my thirties.

For ten long years I struggled to find peace. Sisters and brothers tried to help me, but no matter how hard I fought, I could not break through my dark prison of impurity.

Only through seeing the freedom offered to another member who confessed the sin of lust did it dawn on me that I could find freedom. I realized I had to lower my guard once and for all and reveal myself as the miserable person I was. I had to find someone I could trust and tell them my darkest secrets. I had to repent, and then God would finally give me the peace I had been seeking for so long.

In the next days my whole life flowed in front of my eyes; it was as if I saw every touch, look, word, thought of filth that I had wallowed in, every person I had willfully misled and hurt. With pain, but also with joy, I went to confess my blackest sins to the wife of my pastor. I had to go back many times before I was able to get through everything. Peace poured into my heart after each cleansing. The years seemed to roll off me, and I felt free as a child again.

I'm over forty now, married, with children, but I feel much younger than I did at nineteen. And if someone asked me today, what is peace? I could give them a far better answer.

All of us want to receive new life, and to be changed – that is not the problem. The question is how. As my father writes, "It is God who must change us, and he may do this in a way that upsets our own expectations and ideas, including our plans for inner growth or personal fulfillment. To be fit for God's future, we must be shaped by him."

Rather than accept this, people come up with their own solutions. William, the priest whose story I told earlier, tells me that although he has encountered "every sort and condition of sin" during more than forty years in the ministry, he has seen very little remorse. "More often than not, the guilty rationalize rather than repent."

Most people do not understand what repentance is. Those who do don't like what they see. It is easy enough to set a wrong right by means of an apology, or to shut an eye and gloss things over; people do this every day. Yet that is not repentance. When a soul has been wounded by sin, the only way to healing is through remorse.

At the time of the Reformation, the clergy "forgave" sin through the sale of indulgences. Today, some psychologists and psychiatrists "forgive" sin in the same way. People pay them, and they are told, "You have not done anything wrong; your behavior is quite normal. You don't need to have a bad conscience; you can't help what you have done." That is how the world forgives sin.

In the Gospel of Matthew we find a striking example of true repentance: the story of Peter, who denied Jesus three times the night before the crucifixion. Peter could have defended his action as a forgivable sin. After all, Jesus was in the hands of the authorities, and already sentenced to death. In a sense, there was nothing the disciples could do to change the situation. But instead of making excuses, Peter saw his denial for the cold-hearted betrayal it was. He was cut to the heart, and "went out and wept bitterly."

Repentance is not self-torment; nor does it mean self-centered brooding or depression. But if it is real, it will be painful. Like a plow, repentance tears up the ground, breaks up clods, uproots weeds, and prepares the soil for new planting.

> Lo, all my heart's field red and torn,
> And thou wilt bring the young green corn,
> The young green corn divinely springing,
> The young green corn forever singing...
> And we will walk the weeded field,
> And tell the golden harvest's yield,
> The corn that makes the holy bread
> By which the soul of man is fed,
> The holy bread, the food unpriced,
> Thy everlasting mercy, Christ.
>
> *John Masefield*

Each of us has sinned, and because of this, each of us is in need of such a plowing. In one way or another, we have all bungled our lives. By admitting our faults, we acknowledge our weakness and our dependence on each other and on God. More important, we avoid the danger of drowning out the nagging voice of the burdened conscience. Lasting peace is not found by denying our failures, but by looking at them honestly and squarely.

If the route of repentance is painful, the agony of living with hidden sin is far worse. As Martin Buber has written, the desperate longing for harmony and community with God drives the heart on to peace, like a storm before the calm, and to resist it is to live in a state of constant and terrible tension. "If a man does not judge himself, all things judge him, and all things become messengers of God."

Gerald (not his real name) is an elderly member of our community who sought peace of mind unsuccessfully, year after year. Though deeply sorry for the sins of his past, he had never confessed them fully or truly repented. Gerald was a reliable, hard worker, but inside he was a tortured man. Behind the façade of his steady commitment to church and family life, he carried the secret of an adulterous affair from his youth, and a child from that relationship in a distant city.

In a time of crisis when he was approaching middle age, Gerald was able to consider the true sum of his life up to that point, and at last "God's judgment began to reach my heart." Gerald says he knew there was no way he could "make up for or undo" what he had done, yet when he was able to feel the painful weight of his wrongdoing, he was filled with remorse, and went and humbled himself to every person he had betrayed. Finally, he says, he was able to experience the redemptive cleansing of repentance.

Dramatic as his reckoning was, Gerald says that this experience, and the peace it brought him, was not a one-time event, but a process that continues to this day:

> Many times I thought I had finally found peace, only to realize that what I had found was merely a stepping stone, and that I had to go deeper. This will probably continue. Perhaps it is in the honest pursuit of peace that we find it.

I can say this about the way to peace: I believe it is knowledge of myself and my sinfulness as revealed to me by God's daily judgment. Continuous repentance for the sins I have committed, and gratitude for God's forgiveness. Constant prayer to God to reveal my failures as they come, and to grant me clarity and strength for the tasks of each day. Daily renunciation of all pride, ambition, or anything of self. And daily rejoicing in God, in his gifts and graces, and above all in the miracle of the cross.

The importance of repentance is also shown in the story of my aunt Emy-Margret, a woman who has probably fought a harder fight in her search for peace of heart than anyone I know. When Emy-Margret first met the man who later became her husband, she admired him—like everyone who knew him—for his intelligence, enthusiasm, and charisma. Hans was an articulate and personable businessman, and beyond that, he seemed to care deeply for the welfare of our church, which was young and still developing as a community when he came.

What started as a happy marriage soon evolved into a nightmare. On the outside, things looked great: Hans and Emy-Margret were active members; children arrived, one after the other; and the family seemed to enjoy a wholesome, harmonious life. Privately, however, Hans began to show a different side. He had an insatiable desire for personal power, and seemed willing to go any length to get it, no matter the cost to others or himself.

Emy-Margret was initially troubled by her husband's manipulative style, but this didn't last for long. To criticize Hans meant to open herself to his sarcastic tongue-lashings, and it was much easier—more hassle-free, more comfortable—to accept him as he was. Not that this was entirely pleasant: Hans was mistrustful of almost everyone he lived with, and there were few he hated more than his wife's family, whom he suspected of trying to curtail his influence in the community. It was not long before Hans achieved his aim. Adored by a select few, feared by most, he ruled them all as an effective dictator, and silenced or expelled anyone who questioned or contradicted him.

Decades later Emy-Margret realized that even her own loyalty to her husband had not stopped him from getting what he wanted in life: she discovered that he had carried on an adulterous affair with his secretary for years. Emy-Margret began to cave in. Hans had left her and the community at the time his deceit was revealed, but her emotional dependence on him was so great that it blinded her for years to the irreparable damage they had both caused. Hundreds of members had suffered under their leadership. This bondage, which took the form of a strangely defensive idolization of Hans and everything he stood for, continued even after his tragic death in a dual-jet collision over France.

Yet some time after this, Emy-Margret finally began to see that she had been living a lie; that everything she had hung on to—prestige, power, and the attention of people who admired (or envied) her "social standing"—had gained her no real happiness, but only personal devastation. During the following months she underwent the painful process of sorting out the conflicting loyalties and emotions, pent-up lies and half-lies that had burdened her for decades. It was a long, intense battle, but she struggled to recognize her guilt and set things straight. She begged for—and received—the support of our community.

Decades have now passed since Emy-Margret's fight ended; yet for her and our community, it was a victory whose fruits are still apparent. In worldly terms, her struggle might seem to have been futile. She lost Hans without ever being reconciled to him, she embittered old friends who sided with her husband, and she estranged herself from several of her children in the process.

There is no question that my aunt's quest for peace has cost her much pain. Yet she assures me that in breaking her ties to her husband and repenting she has found a wholeness and healing she never knew before. As she wrote to her brother Hardy some years ago, "Great liberation and peace was given to me and is still being given, far beyond my hopes and prayers."

Bonhoeffer writes that what makes repentance so difficult is its chief requirement: the willingness to die a "painful, shameful death before the eyes of a brother." Because this humiliation is so great, we continually scheme to avoid it. Sometimes, even after we have acknowledged our sins, we try to jump over them (or "manage" them) without truly repenting for them. Yet it is precisely this anguish – this cross – that is our rescue and salvation: "The old man dies, but it is God who has conquered him. Now we share in the resurrection of Christ and eternal life. Having passed through death first, that life will be all the greater."

Conviction

Just because so many things are in conflict does not mean that we ourselves should be divided. Yet time and time again one hears it said that since we have been put into a conflicting world, we have to adapt to it. Oddly, this completely unchristian idea is most often espoused by so-called Christians, of all people.

How can we expect a righteousness to prevail when there is hardly anyone who will give himself up undividedly to a righteous cause? Lately I've thought often of a story from the Old Testament: Moses stood all day and all night with outstretched arms, praying to God for victory. And whenever he let down his arms, the enemy prevailed over the children of Israel. Are there still people today who never weary of directing all their thinking and all their energy, single-heartedly, to one cause?   *Sophie Scholl*

Beheaded by the Nazis in 1943 for her involvement with the White Rose, a Munich-based student group that wrote, printed, and distributed anti-government leaflets, Sophie Scholl was no ordinary twenty-one-year-old. She was no ordinary activist either. In the book *The Resistance of the White Rose*, author Inge Scholl, her sister, remembers the strange peace that accompanied her, and says it was as if Christ was present with her in her darkest hours, guiding her and giving her strength.

When Sophie first came across the White Rose and discovered that her brother Hans was its founder and most active participant, she was angry. At the same time she felt it was a lonely voice for truth and that unless she supported it, it might soon be drowned out by the growing clamor of propaganda and lies. Soon she was throwing all her energy into supporting it.

Several years before, Hans and Sophie had both embraced Hitler's promises of a New Germany with enthusiasm. Yet after they began to realize how many consciences and lives were being trampled by the dictator's demonic lust for power, they grew increasingly determined to swim against the stream. By late 1942 it was hard to find a more vigorous cell of opposition, or a more endangered one.

In February 1943 the leaders of the White Rose were captured and identified, and within five days the Scholls and their closest supporters were dead. Further executions followed in April and July.

The Scholls went to their end bravely, even proudly. When Sophie heard her sentence – death by guillotine – she is said to have reacted calmly: "Such a fine, sunny day, and I have to go. But what does it matter, if through us thousands of others are awakened and stirred to action?" Here was a peace born of unshakable faith.

Today, such conviction is a rare thing. (Who of us cares so deeply about our beliefs that we are willing to be killed for them?) But so is the reassurance and peace it brings in the face of struggle. Unless we are fully convinced of the rightness of what we are doing, we will never be able to face a similar test with such stamina. Perhaps that is the most important thing the White Rose has to teach us.

I am reminded of one of my favorite Old Testament passages: the account of Shadrach, Meshach, and Abednego.

Here were three young men unmatched in their loyalty to God, and in the peace that bore them up when this loyalty was put to the test. The story is well known, but it bears repeating here:

> Then the king said, "If you refuse [to worship my golden statue], you will be thrown into a flaming furnace within the hour. And what god can deliver you out of my hands then?"
>
> Shadrach, Meshach, and Abednego replied, "O Nebuchadnezzar, we are not worried about what will happen to us. If we are thrown into the flaming furnace, our God is able to deliver us; and he will deliver us out of your hand, Your Majesty. But if he doesn't, we will never under any circumstance serve your gods or worship the gold statue you have erected."
>
> Then Nebuchadnezzar was filled with fury and his face became dark with anger at Shadrach, Meshach, and Abednego. He commanded that the furnace be heated up seven times hotter than usual, and called for the strongest of his army to bind the men and throw them into the fire.
>
> So they bound them tight with ropes and threw them into the furnace, fully clothed. And because the king, in his anger, had demanded such a hot fire in the furnace, the flames leaped out and killed the soldiers as they threw them in.
>
> Shadrach, Meshach, and Abednego fell, bound, into the roaring flames. But suddenly, as he was watching, Nebuchadnezzar jumped up in amazement and exclaimed to his advisors, "Didn't we throw three men into the furnace?" "Yes," they said, "we did indeed, Your Majesty." "Well, look!" Nebuchadnezzar shouted. "I see four men – unbound, walking around in the fire, and they aren't even hurt by the flames! And the fourth looks like the son of a god!"
>
> Then Nebuchadnezzar came as close as he could to the open door of the flaming furnace and yelled, "Shadrach, Meshach, and Abednego, servants of the Most High God! Come out! Come here!" So they stepped out of the fire.

Then the princes, governors, captains, and counselors crowded around them and saw that the fire hadn't touched them—not a hair of their heads was singed; their coats were unscorched, and they didn't even smell of smoke!

Then Nebuchadnezzar said, "Blessed be the God of Shadrach, Meshach, and Abednego, for he sent his angel to deliver his trusting servants when they defied the king's commandment and were willing to die rather than serve or worship any god except their own."   *Daniel 3:15–28*

How many "trusting servants" of God are ready to defend the faith today, let alone die for it? How many of us will be turned back from the place of eternal peace, with the words, "I never knew you?"

Looking back over my own life, the men who have influenced me most were those whose convictions cost them their lives. Some I never knew personally (Dietrich Bonhoeffer, Alfred Delp, and Oscar Romero, to name a few). Others, like Martin Luther King, Jr., I was privileged to meet briefly.

My grandfather, a vocal opponent of Hitler's regime, escaped the common fate of most dissidents only because he died in 1935 from complications following an amputation. But according to my grandmother, the possibility of imprisonment only emboldened him. Several times he voluntarily traveled to the Nazi District Office in Kassel, where, once the door was locked behind him, he was allowed to present this or that petition or criticism. Almost miraculously he was given a fair hearing each time and released afterward.

Only days before he died, on Repentance Day (a Lutheran state holiday), my grandfather called out from his hospital bed, so that the whole ward could hear him,

"Has Herr Goebbels repented yet? Has Hitler?" Germans were hauled off to concentration camp for less.

Years later, as a fourteen-year-old in a New York public school, I was inspired by this act of defiance to show my own pluck. The Pledge of Allegiance was recited every day, and each morning a different student took a turn leading it. The day my turn came, I got up in front of the class and told them that I would not do it. My allegiance belonged to God, I said, not to a piece of cloth.

You could have heard a pin drop, my teacher and classmates were so stunned. This was unthinkable! (It was the height of the McCarthy era, and in Washington, the House Un-American Activities Committee hearings were in full swing.) By the end of the morning, I had been reported to the principal and brought before a gathering of the entire faculty to explain myself. Shocked as they were, they showed understanding once I clarified my position and assured them I had meant no disrespect, but had acted only out of my conviction.

At home, my parents were somewhat surprised, though wholly supportive. To my father, it was simple: if you didn't follow your conscience, you would never find peace. If doing this meant rocking the boat, so be it. That was always preferable to sitting back and pretending everything was fine.

In an earlier chapter I mentioned various people I met in my teens, and their influence on me. One of those who stands out most clearly in my mind is Dwight Blough, a young guest from Iowa who later joined our community and became a close confidant of my father's.

Dwight was a man of conviction. He worked hard, played hard, fought hard. He was a man of simplicity, in word and deed. Whatever he did, he did wholeheartedly, and when he had something to say, he got straight to the point. He had no patience for a lot of pious talk.

Norann, Dwight's widow, says he was a typical American teenager, "into all sorts of things," and eager to sign up for the Air Force, which he did at eighteen. During his first year at college, though, Dwight began to long for something more than the predictable course that seemed to lie ahead: a degree, marriage and children, a career, and finally retirement while watching one's children go through the same steps. He felt his life was being turned toward God. By his sophomore year, he had searched and studied the Gospels enough to feel certain that fulfillment could be found only in living for one's fellowmen. On the strength of this conviction he decided that joining the Air Force was wrong, and went about having his status changed.

In the next three years, Dwight and Norann married, found out about our community, visited, and asked to stay. Dwight taught in our school, but it wasn't long before his gifts as a pastor were recognized and affirmed. Not that he was a saint. Sometimes his zeal was impulsive, and his tendency to choose honesty over diplomacy could make the sparks fly. So did his preference for action over consideration.

I'll never forget the terrible day our community's main building burned down, in the winter of 1957, and the speed with which Dwight found a ladder and appeared in a top-floor window. Smoke and flames stopped him before he got his hands on the things he hoped to save, but he had tried. The rest of us had stayed on the ground, shouting at him to get down before it was too late. It was the same when there was an accident, or when someone became seriously sick. Dwight was usually the first person there.

In the early 1970s our communities bought a plane to ease travel between them, and Dwight's enthusiasm extended to aviation as well.

On December 30, 1974 Dwight was killed when a plane he was copiloting crashed on a foggy mountainside. Norann was left widowed with twelve children, the youngest only seven weeks old. Among her husband's papers she found notes for his next sermon on the theme of conviction and readiness.

Dwight's death was a tremendous blow to everyone in our communities, and a wake-up call for each of us who knew him. He had been taken unexpectedly and suddenly, at the age of forty. What about the rest of us? Were we ready to die?

As I think about the question now, decades later, it seems every bit as immediate as it did then. For what else is peace with God, if not readiness to meet him? If peace is readiness, it must mean readiness in every aspect of our lives: readiness to forgive the unforgivable; to remember when we would sooner forget, to forget when we would rather remember. It means readiness to love when we have hated; to go where we would rather not go, and to wait if we have been forgotten; to look forward, not back; to draw a line under the past and turn toward the light. It means readiness to give everything and to lay down our life for our brother.

As far as Dwight was concerned, the answer was clear. He had lived life to the full. And in a manner that later seemed uncannily prophetic, he had spoken of his readiness to go to God not only in his last notes, but also in a pastoral letter two months before:

Jesus' words, "If you love me, you will keep my commandments," are so very vital for us just now when the world is racing into such immorality, mammonism, and sin...I feel such a call to be more radical in my obeying and following Jesus. We often say that the world will know we belong to Jesus only if we are completely united and love each other. If that is so, then our love must become much stronger toward Christ and our brothers and sisters, and all people!

And I must also repent ever more deeply for wherever I have stood in the way, or been lukewarm, halfhearted, narrow-minded, or self-centered...

All selfishness, opinionatedness, and pride must be given up and overcome so that we can live solely for Christ, his cause, his mission, his future, and his kingdom here on earth.

Jesus said, "This is my commandment, that you love one another as I have loved you. Greater love has no man than this, that a man lay down his life for his friends. You are my friends if you do what I command you." The earliest believers had this love to one another and to Christ. Do we?

In closing, Dwight quoted the following words from my grandfather—a favorite passage of his:

To be ready is everything! Therefore the expectation of God's coming must be our active readiness, so that we stretch out our hands to him, ready to be crucified with him; so that we fall on our knees, ready to be humbled by him; and so that we lay down all our own power, that he alone may have power over us. *Let us be ready!*

Realism

Have the patience and courage to begin anew each day, and trust in God's help; his mercy is new every morning. Then you will understand that life is a matter of becoming or growing, and that you must look forward to greater things. Even though you stand in battle with dark powers, victory will be yours, since in Christ every evil is overcome. You will always remain at the beginning of your search, because you will continually change, yet in faith you will find the fulfillment of all your longing.

Eberhard Arnold

Without forgiveness and the possibility of a new start each day, we might be tempted to give up the search for peace as a futile exercise. Conversion can make us new men and women; prayer, humility, repentance, and all the rest can keep us on the right path. Yet ultimately, our hope for peace must be tempered by our recognition of human imperfectibility. Unless we reconcile ourselves to this reality and turn to Christ, the only sinless man, we will remain frustrated forever.

Art Wiser, a long-time member of my church, recently wrote to me:

Have I found peace? I'm not *at* peace. When I'm in the wrong, and someone points it out to me, I'm in turmoil for a bit and often struggle against myself; I lose sleep; I have butterflies. Yet Jesus said, "I give you my peace." And in spite of my sinfulness and willfulness, I am following him, so I accept his word with joy. The same evening Jesus said this, he was "troubled in spirit"; later he suffered agony in the Garden of Gethsemane. If he suffered like that for our sake, who am I to be questioning his peace in me? I accept it, I affirm it, even as I long and pray for it. His peace is a part of the unending battle for his kingdom.

The tension Art speaks of is a natural part of life. All of us have mood swings and bad days, and it is foolish to hope that we will ever overcome them completely. Yet as Arlene, another member of my church, notes in the following letter, the knowledge that God is in control gives us a security we can return to over and over. Like a rudder, it can set us on course whenever anxieties threaten our stability.

> When I become frantic or overly concerned about anything, no matter how important or kingdom-oriented, I lose my sense of inner calm. When things don't go my way, or something happens that frustrates me, when plans or ideas about how things should be are disturbed—even when I pray, if I am overly self-concerned—I lose peace. Inner peace comes by completely trusting God.
>
> Whenever we feel the urge to take on God's work, it is a sign that we have lost trust in him, and forgotten that he is in control. It doesn't matter whether it is something in our personal or family life, something we hear on the news, something we experience in our work. If we try to solve everything ourselves, we become restless, discouraged, flustered, anxious. We lose the peace of God.

The struggle Arlene describes will be familiar to every person who is actively engaged in trying to change the world in some way, whether by working for justice or peace or any other ideal. In a sense, it is a fruitless struggle. Swiss writer Friedrich Dürrenmatt has pointed out that we cannot, as single human beings, save the world: "that it would be as hopeless an endeavor as that of poor Sisyphus." In any case, he goes on, this task has not been laid in our hands, nor in the hands of a power, a people, "or even the devil, who is the mightiest of these. It lies in the hand of God, whose will stands alone." Therefore the following advice:

> In the face of the strain of tasks beyond our strength, we must turn inwards to the Source of strength. If we measure our human strength against the work we see immediately ahead, we shall feel hopeless, and if we tackle it in that strength we shall be frustrated...and fall either into torpor or exasperation. There is no healthier lesson we can learn than our own limitations, provided this is accompanied by the resignation of our own strength and reliance on the strength of God. The wheel of life will fly apart unless it is spoked to the Center, and we are placing ourselves in danger whenever we fail to recognize this, whenever we go rushing onward without taking time to turn inward.   *Philip Britts*

In the tumultuous time of the Reformation, even the Anabaptists — the era's most relentless voices for change — realized this. These fearless men and women tried to change the world from the bottom up, by unmasking the hypocrisy of the established church, by defying the authority of the state, and by overturning the most sacred social conventions. Yet despite their zeal, their faith was realistic. They did not suffer from the illusion that some gentle world springtime was on the way; they knew all too well what their faith would cost them. At the same time, certain as they were of their fate, they were also sure that God would one day be victorious. And when persecution came, with rack and stake, dungeon and sword, they struggled on unbowed.

For us who live in a time when our efforts for peace cost us very little, the Anabaptists have much to teach us. Like them, we must come to see that it is not important how effective or successful we are, but whether we carry out our tasks with an attitude of faith. A few years before he died, my father said in this regard:

> There is such endless need on earth, much more than we can ever know. Some of it is economic need, and some of it is social need, but in a deeper way it is all inner need brought into people's lives by the dark powers of injustice, murder, and unfaithfulness. Some of us used to believe that through political or social measures radical changes could take place in our society – changes that would answer this need. But as we have seen time and again the state always gets caught in its own web of dishonesty; the cold dollar rules, and selfishness and unfaithfulness are everywhere.
>
> We know that by ourselves we cannot change the world. But Christ will, and we want to give ourselves voluntarily to him. He demands our whole personality and our whole life. He came to save the world, and we believe that he, not any human leader, will one day govern the earth. For him we live, and for him we are willing to die. That is all that is asked of anyone. Jesus does not expect perfection, but he expects us to serve him wholeheartedly.

To serve Christ in this way does not mean running oneself ragged. If we view the world through an idealistic lens, the peace we are looking for will always be perfect and unbroken – and faraway. If we are realistic, we will be more willing to accept the fact that the peace we can enjoy on this earth has limits, and we will be more objective in discerning our priorities.

Take prayer, for example. One common blind spot is the idea that we are achieving more when we are "doing" something. In actual fact, the fruits of prayer, silence, contemplation, or meditation, even if not tangible, are just as significant as those of the most heroic "active" fight. In his book *Blessed Are the Meek*, South African Archbishop Desmond Tutu reminds us that as we strive for peace, we should not forget that the hidden prayers "offered by nuns, by contemplatives, by old women and old men, by the sick in hospitals" make up a "crucial part of our struggle," one every bit as noteworthy as the more visible activity carried out on the front lines by the young and the physically strong.

Benedict Groeschel, a close friend, leads a busy life of prayer *and* action—serving the poor and the homeless in the Bronx, speaking out against abortion, and leading a small household of Franciscan friars. A scholar and priest, Father Benedict took his vows when he was seventeen. Now an old man, he remains refreshingly down-to-earth. And though he works unstintingly, he never seems burned out. He is realistic about his goals, and comfortable with his limitations. In a recent conversation he said:

> I think peace comes from faith, hope, and charity. But it's not simply a feeling. Peace helps us to go on in the struggle of life. Remember, I'm from Jersey City, and the light at the end of the tunnel in Jersey City is Hoboken. We're not optimists. We are not people who go through this life thinking it's all wonderful. We know that it's a valley of tears. So we don't have any great expectations of this world. And consequently, things that bother other people don't bother us so much.
>
> I always find great consolation in the Book of Job. I love those beautiful verses: "Where were you when I laid the foundation of the earth? Tell me, if you have understanding… Can you bind the chains of the Pleiades, or loose the cords of Orion? Can you guide the Bear with its children? Do you know the ordinances of the heavens? Can you establish their rule on the earth? Tell me."

There's a certain humor in this Book. You know, how everything goes wrong? Everything? It's like this:

"How're you doing?"

"The worst day of my life."

"How is everything going?"

"Everything is going wrong. Everything! Nothing is not going wrong."

We have this with Saint Paul too: "For the love of Christ I am put to death all the day long." It's so Jewish. If he were an Englishman he would have said, "Well, it was somewhat unpleasant, you know; somewhat unpleasant. A fair amount of difficulty, you know."

I have these Jewish friends. They say to me, "You come in here every day and never ask me how I am!"

"I'm sorry," I say. "How are you?"

"Don't ask!"

Benedict has been jailed more than once because of his pro-life activities, and when I asked him about it, he said:

Well, the first time I was jailed it was delightful because I was just there for part of a day. I said my prayers, made a meditation, took a nap. It was delightful. The next time I was there, it was appalling. I have always been nice to correctional personnel; and when people give them a hard time I tell them, "Don't do that. These guys are just trying to earn a living."

But then I saw how terribly they treated the inmates. For some reason, an otherwise perfectly decent man who is a prison guard will suddenly treat everybody like an animal...

It was awful. I was strip-searched three times in twenty-four hours. And the only people who were kind were the prison doctor and the prisoners. The prisoners were very civil. They didn't know I was clergy, but they called me Pop. When I was coming out they gave me my habit back, and I was in a big room with prisoners about to be released. You would not have believed the language in there. But they didn't mean to be disrespectful. They didn't know it was wrong.

SEEKING PEACE

When they saw me get my robe back, they said, "What are you doing in here, Reverend?" I told them I was here for picketing an abortion clinic, and they were all outraged. But one old gentleman, an old black man, stood up, and said to the prisoners, "No, it's right. He *should* be in jail!"

"Shut up, man! Sit down!"

"But it's right."

"Why is it right?"

"Because Jesus says in the gospels, 'Blessed are they that suffer persecution for righteousness' sake.'"

Well, that was a slap in the face to stop feeling sorry for myself. Because there was the Word of the Lord delivered right there by a prisoner!

Father Benedict went on to speak of Christ's crucifixion and its significance especially for those who want peace but are not willing to work for it. People are unrealistic, he said; they want the paycheck without the job, victory without struggle. Paraphrasing Cardinal Newman, he continued:

The crucifixion of Christ puts a value and meaning on everything in the world, the good, the bad, riches, poverty, suffering, joy, sorrow, pain. They all come together at the cross. Of course, after the crucifixion comes the resurrection. But if you speak of the second without the first — that's phony.

There are many people who would like to skip the crucifixion and get straight to the resurrection, but it doesn't work. They will commute back.

168

Service

This is the true joy of life: being used up for a
purpose recognized by yourself as a mighty one;
being a force of nature instead of a feverish,
selfish little clod of ailments and grievances,
complaining that the world will not devote
itself to making you happy.

I am of the opinion that my life belongs to
others, and as long as I live, it is my privilege
to do for them whatever I can. I want to be
thoroughly used up when I die, for the harder I
work, the more I live...

Life is no brief candle to me. It is a sort of
splendid torch which I have got hold of for a
moment, and I want to make it burn as brightly
as possible before handing it on to future generations.   *George Bernard Shaw*

Of all the roots of unpeace, the most widespread is probably selfishness, whether within ourselves, in our relationships with others, or in the world at large. It may also
be the hardest to weed out. Problems such as arrogance,
mistrust, anger, or resentment can be addressed in a fairly
straightforward fashion; we can usually take specific steps
to uncover their cause and to overcome them. But selfishness is often simply there, unnamed, unnoticed, yet so
powerful and deep-seated that it shapes our entire outlook
on life.

Sometimes selfishness takes the form of an obvious sin,
such as lust or greed. At other times, as in the case of an

egocentric search for personal happiness or holiness, it may take such a "harmless" form that we are unaware of its danger. Once selfishness is recognized for what it is, however, there is a simple and universal antidote for it: service to others.

Service, in the words of sixteenth-century mystic Teresa of Avila, is the act of being God to each other: "God has no hands, nor has he feet nor voice except ours; and through these he works." Growing up in a large family on a farm where everyone had to work hard, I never heard anyone talk about service in this way, but looking back I am sure my parents must have viewed it with similar reverence.

Certainly we were taught its importance. From early on I remember my father's emphasis on the fact that Jesus, the "suffering servant," identified with the downtrodden and the poor; that he chose a donkey (not a horse) for his triumphal entry into Jerusalem; that he welcomed children, visited the bedridden, healed the sick, and talked with common sinners; finally, that he stooped to wash the feet of his followers. But service was not preached as a virtue. It was simply practiced.

When the only job my father could find was gardening in a leper colony, he made nothing of it. It could have meant contracting the disease and ending up there permanently, but he never told us children that. He said only that there was honor in doing the humblest service for others, and doing it gladly.

As for my mother, she was always on the run, bringing an elderly neighbor or a new mother a bouquet of flowers or a jar of preserves; missing a meal to sit with someone who was sick; getting up early to write to a lonely person or to finish knitting a gift.

In later years I was impressed by the service I saw at places like the Catholic Worker, where volunteers made sandwiches and soup, swept floors, and spent long hours listening to the problems of the homeless and needy, who were not always grateful guests.

Ruth Land, a member of my church and a former doctor, says it is this sort of modest service that brings her the greatest satisfaction:

> You can look everywhere for peace, but you may not find it. Or you can forget yourself and get on with whatever work is there in front of you. That's what brings peace–doing whatever needs to be done in the house, showing love to your spouse, or whatever else comes to mind. If you do it for the sake of the kingdom, it will bring you peace.

An Indian story retold by Gandhi touches on a similar truth: the little kindnesses we show to others are just as important as our nobler achievements. A troubled woman came to her guru, saying, "O master, I find that I cannot serve God." He asked, "Is there nothing, then, that you love?" She responded, "My little nephew." And he said to her, "There is your service to God, in your love to that child."

Sometimes the greatest service is the least noticed. In my community many elderly members work several hours a day, folding clothes in our laundry, classifying books in our library, or helping in our wood and metal shops. In every case, the service they perform is invaluable, and not only in terms of what is produced. The sense of well-being and peace it gives them, and the joy that shines in their eyes when they speak about it, enriches our common life in a wonderful way.

Joe Bush, a friend who suffers from Parkinson's disease, was once a capable gardener. Now his activity is limited to sitting at a desk for a few hours each day, where he slowly progresses on a long translation project, one painstaking keystroke after another. Others might be frustrated, but not Joe.

> My work is pure joy. Speaking of which, I'd like to mention something that comes to mind regarding work. In another church I used to attend, the minister kept mentioning all the rewards we would get for working hard and being faithful. It was as though he believed we each have a credit balance in heaven. I do not subscribe to this idea at all.
>
> If anything, I have a big debt…I shall die a sinner, though one who has tried to repent every day for quite some time. But I can't worry about that. I have work to do, a service to perform, and I want to continue to do it and leave the rest to God, trusting in him and looking to the day when his kingdom shall come on this most wonderful and beautiful world which he has made.

Audrey, Joe's wife, finds the same peace in serving others:

> Joe and I may be nearing the end of our mortal lives, but there is all eternity before us, and that is a most exciting thought. And when we say "No thank you, I can manage," to those who care for us—half blind and lame as we are—it is not that we are ungrateful. It is just that life is more exciting if we can use ourselves up as long as we can. A tall candle does not suddenly go out when there is only an inch left; it burns on until there is just a little puddle of wax to show where it has been. There is still lots for us to do.
>
> Even when we are no longer able to do anything useful at all, we can pray for those who can. And we can take comfort in that last line from Milton's sonnet, "On His Blindness," which he wrote at the end of his life after he had lost his sight: "They also serve, who only stand and wait."

Both Joe and Audrey say that their tasks are meaningful because they serve a purpose. A job is never just a job; nor is work, if it does this. Without a purpose, work can be as meaningless, and create as much frustration and despair, as unemployment or enforced inactivity. According to Viktor Frankl, the same is true of life in general:

> I have repeatedly seen that an appeal to continue life, to survive the most unfavorable conditions, can be made only when such survival appears to have a meaning. That meaning must be specific and personal, a meaning which can be realized by this one person alone and bring him peace of mind. For we must never forget that every person is unique in the universe.
>
> I remember my dilemma in a concentration camp when faced with a man and a woman who were close to suicide. Both had told me that they expected nothing more from life. I asked both my fellow prisoners whether the question was really what we expected from life. Was it not, rather, what life was expecting from us? I suggested that life was awaiting something from them. In fact, the woman was being awaited by her child abroad, and the man had a series of books he had begun to write and publish but had not yet finished.
>
> I have said that man should not ask what he may expect from life, but should rather understand that life expects something from him. It may also be put this way: in the last resort, man should not ask, "What is the meaning of my life?" but should realize that he himself is being questioned. Life is putting its problems to him, and it is up to him to respond to these questions by being responsible; he can only answer to life by answering for *his* life.
>
> Life is a task. The religious person differs from the apparently irreligious only by experiencing his existence not simply as a task, but as a mission. This means that he is also aware of the Taskmaster, the source of his mission. For thousands of years that source has been called God.

Looked at in this way, life provides us with a wonderful purpose: to make the fullest use of it by serving others, so that we are prepared to meet God when death comes. I have been at the bedsides of many dying people, and it is obvious that some die in peace, and others in torment. The difference seems to lie in the way they spent their lives. Did they give their lives in service, or did they live selfishly? In the end, the only thing that matters is one's relationship to one's fellow human beings and to God.

To live selfishly is to be constantly aware of what we must give up, even if we do make sacrifices here and there. We end up seeing everything in terms of how it affects us. It is a way of life that yields precious little peace. Service to others saves us from this predicament, because it reminds us of what we are living *for* and helps us forget ourselves. It also gives us a new perspective – one that allows us to see the size of our life in relation to the rest of the universe.

True service is always an act of showing another person love. It is easy to forget this, even in a religious community like my own, where service is at the core of every member's commitment. Whenever we let our work become an end in itself, we lose sight of the love that gives it a deeper purpose, and gradually it becomes a mindless, mechanical chore. With love, the most mundane task can take on meaning. Without it, the noblest task can become drudgery.

Some time ago I visited Plum Village, Thich Nhat Hanh's Buddhist community in France. One thing that struck me was the way residents nurture an awareness of work as service.

There is always plenty to do at Plum Village, what with new buildings going up, renovations to be made on old houses, and several large orchards to maintain. Yet work for its own sake is frowned on. Rather than accepting the usual western emphasis on what must be accomplished during the course of the day, the people of Plum Village cultivate the ideal of "living in the present." They try to see each situation, each action, each encounter with another human being as an opportunity to become "more fully alive." Karl Riedl, a resident, explained to me:

> The art of working in mindfulness helps us to reconsider the whole idea of being effective. It helps us question our obsession with goals and our idea that everything must be done "just so." It makes us look in a new light at the images we have of ourselves as good or not good at certain tasks, and helps uncover and recover the joy that should inspire everything we do—whether working in the greenhouse, chopping wood, cleaning toilets, writing, or hanging out the wash. All too often, we do not work mindfully, and we let our busyness shatter our harmony and happiness.

A verse from the commune's chanting book sheds further light on this attitude and reveals its priorities, at least as far as service is concerned:

> I vow to offer joy to one person in the morning
> And to relieve the grief of one person in the afternoon.
> I vow to live simply and sanely,
> Content with few possessions.
> I vow to keep my body healthy.
> I vow to let go of all worries and anxieties
> In order to be light and free.

Skeptics might disparage this understanding of work as high-minded or unnaturally self-conscious. But they, as we all, would do well to remember that it is service, more than anything else, that gives hands and feet to the Gospels. Service is the essence of what Jesus taught—Jesus, who promises us that if we follow in his steps, he will give us the peace that passes understanding.

> Christ does not save all those who say to him: Lord, Lord. But he saves all those who out of a pure heart give a piece of

bread to a starving man, without thinking about him the least little bit. And these, when he thanks them, reply: Lord, when did we feed thee?...An atheist and an "infidel," capable of pure compassion, are as close to God as is a Christian, and consequently know him equally well, although their knowledge is expressed in different words, or remains unspoken. For "God is love."   *Simone Weil*

V

The Abundant Life

"We look at life and cannot
untangle the eternal song:
Rings and knots of joy and grief
all laced and interlocking."

The Ramayana

The Abundant Life

We will never arrive at a perfect state of peace, or find it once and for all. We can follow the stepping stones across the water as cautiously and earnestly as we like, but on the other side we will still be ourselves.

All the same, there is no question that once we experience peace, our hearts are opened to a new dimension of living. In a sense, that new dimension is much more than a matter of peace. It is the new existence promised us by Jesus when he said, "I have come to bring you life, that you may have it abundantly."

Several of the people who contributed to this book told me it was this verse more than anything else that set them on their journeys. To seek for peace as an end in itself, they said, was too self-serving an exercise: "Now I've found peace. What next?"

As for the "abundant" life, they said this best described what they are looking for, and not only for themselves – a life of freedom and joy, commitment, compassion, justice, and unity. Not a life without tears and suffering, yet one in which these find their place against the mighty backdrop of the kingdom of God, where perfect peace shall reign.

Josef Ben-Eliezer, a European of Jewish descent, came to our community many years ago in search of such a life, though as an atheist at the time, he would not have described it that way:

> What motivated my searching was the hatred and bloodshed I saw in my childhood and youth, especially during World War II, when my family fled from Germany to Poland, then to Siberia, and finally to Israel. I felt peace could be found only in the context of an answer to the universal need for brotherhood, and that is what drove me to seek it.

I was involved in the national liberation movement in
Israel, and the conflicts that it entailed, but turned away from
it after I experienced that, in coming to power, this movement became an oppressive one. Then I looked for an answer
in world revolution. I studied Marx, Lenin, and Trotsky, and
later, in Paris, I became involved in various leftist causes. But
a nagging question occupied me more and more: where is the
guarantee that if the revolution is victorious, those who gain
power will not end up oppressing the masses themselves, as
happened in Russia and elsewhere?

Joining the church where I am now a member and reading
about the early Christians, who inspired its communal way
of life, I was struck by something new. I saw that the early
church was a truly revolutionary movement, proclaiming a
new order and living it. And though Jesus was the center of
their life, it was not the Jesus of conventional Christianity, but
the real, historical Son of God, who has power to overcome
division between person and person, nation and nation...

I found a unity of heart I had longed for over many years. I
believe this unity is every person's longing. To be sure, there
needs to be a change of heart before it can be given. That is
why Jesus called us to repent, to turn our lives upside down.
I experienced that as well, and continue to experience it. But
Jesus did not teach us to look for a peaceful state of mind for
ourselves. He said, "Seek first the kingdom of God."

In his book *Innerland*, my grandfather speaks of the search
for peace in a similar way, and says that though many
believe they will find peace by seeking their own happiness,
this is a false idea. Peace is not the same thing as emotional
gratification, he writes; it is also more than individual bliss.
"It was a completely different urge that set me on the way
of discipleship; namely, the call that reveals God's will
in following Christ; the call that, coming from the place
of his future reign, sets justice and honor above personal
comfort..."

True peace, he goes on, must mean more than contentment of soul. Certainly fellowship with Christ and with others demands that a person be at peace within himself. But it must go further. It means being freed from division, for it is "a fruit of the divine will to unity, and through it all conditions and relationships, all things and actions, are brought into the redemptive light of God's kingdom."

Jane Clement, a writer and long-time member of our community, says she sought peace of mind for many years, but found it only when she gave up the search and centered her life on something greater than herself.

> In the steady process of turning away from self, we become reliant upon God. We seek for the advancement of the kingdom, not of ourselves. Our goal is not self-discipline but the harmonious functioning of the community around us...For me it was a great freeing to see myself as unimportant, for this very realization brought with it the tranquility and inner reconciliation I had previously sought through self-examination and over-conscientiousness.

Few of us experience such a freeing. We are resigned to disunity and unpeace; it's "just the way things are," and we forget what riches God has in store for us. Only rarely do we catch a glimpse of his greatness. Most of the time the distractions of day-to-day life, as well as our own stupidity and dullness, keep us from seeing farther than the ends of our noses. If we do seek peace, we tend to go after it selfishly.

Writing of the search for peace in his own life, Thomas Merton suggests that it must go hand in hand with what he calls the "openness of love."

> When I came to this monastery where I am, I came in revolt against the meaningless confusion of a life in which there was so much activity, so much movement, so much useless talk,

so much superficial and needless stimulation, that I could not remember who I was. But the fact remains that my flight from the world is not a reproach to you who remain in the world, and I have no right to repudiate the world in a purely negative fashion, because if I do that my flight will have taken me not to truth and to God but to a private, though doubtless pious, illusion…

The contemplative life is the search for peace, but not in an abstract exclusion of all outside reality, not in a barren, negative closing of the senses upon the world, but in the openness of love.

Mary Wiser, a member of our community, began to search for the meaning of life when she was still a child. She soon found that it involved far more than peace of mind and the attainment of personal happiness:

There has been a thread running all through my life that has kept me seeking for the kingdom. Since my childhood I have loved this earth, and I have always been (and am) very attached to those I love, but I can't remember a time when I did not know that there was a land brighter, more vibrant and living than this one, and that I belonged to it.

Very early I was aware of the words of Jesus, "Seek ye first the kingdom of heaven…" and "He who does not hate father and mother…" I felt that Jesus was calling me. But I was also keenly aware of my parents' conviction that the highest form of love and happiness was to live for one's family. I watched the sleepy middle-aged people in church who sang, "Faith of our fathers…could we like them die for Thee." Did they know what they were saying? I joined the church at twelve years, and was surprised and puzzled that nobody seemed to think it meant very much. The camp meetings of the Free Methodists both pulled and repelled me.

And war? I was born in 1918 just as World War I ended, in a seemingly secure corner of rural New York. Yet some of my earliest memories are of listening to veterans tell of their experiences in France. One day a playmate and I discovered in her grandmother's parlor a set of stereopticon pictures of trench fighting. I was incredulous: ordinary people whom I knew had actually killed other people!

Our Methodist Sunday School had an active series on peace issues, and I drank it in. In high school I did research on the causes of war. Nobody else was interested.

My father would have wanted me to follow the usual course—a good college, a secure job, the establishment. But by the end of high school my thoughts were wandering far afield from my small-town, Republican milieu: I was hungry for life. "I have come that you may have life, and have it more abundantly!" These words resonated in my heart.

Mary received a scholarship to Cornell and discovered the wide horizons of a world influenced by secular humanism, progressive politics, and liberal sexual mores. She also found a lively circle of friends on campus who felt the way she did about racism and war.

We were quite radical for that day and age. It was the time of the Spanish Civil War, and Hitler was beginning to flex his muscles. We had to think through our pacifism. Our group became smaller.

During the first term of my senior year I went through a period of depression for the first time in my life. I had gradually severed myself from my basic belief in Jesus, and though I still held to the social gospel, I had lost my childlike peace. I could not find it again.

After a stint teaching in a high school near Ithaca, Mary met Art, a staunch pacifist and anti-war activist. She married him, "even though I had never heard of conscientious objectors until I went to college." After they were married, she was surprised to find out that he did not believe in

God, but she trusted his integrity and his reverence for the Sermon on the Mount.

> The next years, 1941–1945, tried our souls, as was the fate of our whole generation. In that "last good war" there was much contempt for C.O.'s like my husband, who refused to help stop Hitler. We suffered with friends who went off to the war, too, and the terrible suffering of millions in war-torn lands across the sea was ever in our consciousness. My old Methodist church now had an American flag alongside the pulpit, and I never went inside the little building again.

Like most war resisters, Art was interned during the war. He was sent to a Civilian Public Service camp in North Dakota. Mary moved west to be near him, and found work in a one-room schoolhouse. Anti-German sentiment was strong, and pacifists were not welcome.

> One night the parents of the children I taught ganged up on me at the school, where I lived as well as taught. Luckily they soon calmed down and concluded that it was my "coward" husband in the C.P.S. camp nearby whom they were really angry with…
>
> Toward the end of the war Art felt he had to protest the whole war machine – he wanted no part of it any longer – and walked out of camp. He was promptly arrested and imprisoned for several months.
>
> We shared those years with several other couples who were looking for a life of simple integrity, a way to live that would begin eliminating the causes of war. We decided to study community. Later we settled with some of the same people in a community in northern Georgia. But as we lived together it became painfully clear that we were out of our depth in coping with evil, and disunited in our beliefs and ideas. It was a time of sifting.
>
> Art and I experienced much of the "kingdom spirit" in friends and in various worthy causes, whether Christian or

not, and much good in "good" human beings. But we were
blind to the King of the kingdom, the only power that can
cope with the evil in society, which is also in every human
being. Eventually I realized that I had always tried to figure
Jesus out with my head. I had never stopped to ask him who
he was. Once I did, it was wonderful to discover how quickly
I could believe.

Later I described my experience to Heinrich, a close
friend. I will never forget his response: "That is just what
happened to me, only I was also judged." I was overcome by
his humility. And I knew then that I needed – and longed – to
be judged too.

Looking back, Mary sees the significance of repentance as
never before:

I see now that I opposed the kingdom with my good self-
image and my ambition to be used by God. I appropriated
the good things God had given to me, and was not willing
to expose my rebellious heart. The light had to penetrate the
crevices of my heart before it could touch that evil, and to
my shame it took a long time. But with the help of brothers
and sisters I wrestled until the outside and the inside were the
same, and a wonderful freedom came to me.

I don't think my values have shifted radically from my
youth, but they have deepened – from idealism, e.g. the
brotherhood of man – to a real life *lived* with brothers and
sisters committed to each other for good. Jesus' last prayer,
"May they all be one, Father, as thou art one with me," is
my anchor and my joy. Prayer is increasingly a wonder to
me, and a responsibility, I think, now that I can no longer do
much active work.

Yes, I know the peace that Jesus gives. But it is not an
unbroken serenity. There are still times of struggle. To
me, peace means the fight of the Spirit to conquer all lands,
including the inner land of the invisible, with the weapon

of love, to win them over to God. To experience this peace and prize it as the pearl of great price is what gives my life meaning.

When I consider that the battle for the kingdom is universe-wide, I am awed, especially by the coming of God's Son, Jesus, to this earth, and by his sticking with us through our petty struggles. I am convinced that our individual stories belong to this fight too, for they are God's doing. And I look tremblingly to eternity as a continuation of God's wonderful story. Somehow I believe it will continue to unfold.

Mary's thoughts take us far beyond the quest for peace of mind, back to the paradoxical truth that only those who lose their lives will find it. Those who give up their life so completely for the sake of the kingdom that even their search for personal fulfillment becomes unimportant, will be given it back a hundredfold.

Our life will become not narrower, but broader; not more limited, but more boundless; not more regulated, but more abundant; not more pedantic, but more bounteous; not more sober, but more enthusiastic; not more faint-hearted, but more daring; not more empty and human, but more filled by God; not sadder, but happier; not more incapable, but more creative. All this is Jesus and his spirit of freedom and peace. He is coming to us. Let us go into his future radiant with joy!   *Eberhard Arnold*

Security

I don't gather that God wants us to pretend
our fear doesn't exist, to deny it, or evis-
cerate it. Fear is a reminder that we are crea-
tures – fragile, vulnerable, totally dependent on
God. But fear shouldn't dominate or control or
define us. Rather, it should submit to faith and
love. Otherwise, fear can make us unbelieving,
slavish, and inhuman.

I have seen that struggle: containing my
fear, rejecting its rule, recognizing that it saw
only appearances, while faith and love saw substance, saw reality, saw God's bailiwick, so to
speak: "Take courage, it is I. Do not be afraid!"

Philip Berrigan

Twice in my life I had the privilege of meeting Mother
Teresa, and both times I was struck by the same thing: her
quiet confidence. Mother Teresa will go down in history
first and foremost for her work with Calcutta's destitute
and dying, and that is fitting. But anyone who has spent
time serving the poor knows that good deeds alone do not
bring fulfillment. In fact, many who give themselves in this
way receive only frustration and weariness for their efforts.
Mother Teresa's calm was rooted in something deeper than
her work: a sense of security in her calling, and an assurance of her place in life.

Security can be many things: confidence, freedom from
fear, the absence of worry and self-doubt. It also implies
a knowledge of our goals, our identity, and our purpose

in the world. In Mother Teresa, this sense of purpose was especially strong. To use her own analogy, she saw herself as a pencil in the hand of God. This gave her strength no matter how much criticism and slander came her way.

People today lack a strong identity; as Kierkegaard noted a century ago, they are afraid not only to hold an opposing opinion, but to hold an opinion at all. Is it any wonder that so few find peace? I am not suggesting that we should attempt to imitate the zeal and commitment of a Mother Teresa. Different people have different callings, and more often than not, the road to peace is long and hard, with unexpected twists and turns. Yet the inward stability that comes to someone who feels confident before God should not be underestimated. Such a person has a security no one can take away, and it is a fruit of peace.

Freda Dyroff left her native England to come to our community in Germany in the 1930s. Outwardly there was little that was appealing. Joining meant accepting extreme poverty, learning a foreign language and customs, and moving to a country that was headed for war with her own. Yet Freda was confident she had chosen the right path:

> Nothing material attracted me – it was the certainty of a calling that brought battles but promised peace. The community was desperately poor, and life was hard and rough. But that didn't deter me. Here were men and women living in harmony in a world that was going to pieces. They were living a solution: they had abolished class distinctions and social inequalities by abandoning private property and pooling everything. No one owned anything, and everyone shared what they had. And it was not just a vision, something to read about, as in the Book of Acts. It was real.
>
> I joined, and in doing so I finally felt that God's peace, which I had sought for so many years – teaching, working in

the London slums, and doing other things—was with me. Of course I had to give up many things to gain this peace: my house, home, family and friends; my country, my language, the comforts of a bourgeois life, and so on.

No one could understand why I was doing this, and I was amazed and hurt at the enmity and even hatred that came from those closest to me. Later I discovered I had to give up much more: my individualism (though never my conscience), my self-will, and many of my strong opinions.

In return I found great and undeserved love, and the peace Jesus speaks of, which is the assurance that God will see me through everything, including death. I have lived through shaking events—the horror of the Second World War, and a hazardous crossing to South America at the height of the Battle of the Atlantic, during which my first child was born. There were situations of extreme danger, and fear sometimes gripped my heart. Yet underneath I always felt a strange sense of inward calm, a trust in God. Whom else could I trust? This peace came from knowing that even if I was in danger, God's will would be done. Each of us was in his hands.

All these situations did not just "happen." Life does not just happen; nor does peace drop into your lap. There is always struggle, and there are always choices to be made.

To go back to my youth: it took me years to find peace. I wavered between serving God and serving mammon, and my vacillations brought me no rest. I imagine all young adults go through such experiences of longing and frustration, even great turmoil. But I know what helped me, and I can advise others to do the same: seek! Seek until you find, and don't give up. Pray, too, even if you think you don't believe, because God hears even the "unbeliever" as she groans. God will help you through. Don't give up, and above all, avoid the temptations that distract you from what you know you really long for. If you do fall, pick yourself up again and get back on track.

Like most things in life, security is not a constant. It is a fruit of peace—that is certain—but it does not guarantee the absence of struggle or fear. Rather, it is confidence that these things can and will be overcome. My grandfather writes:

> The world alarms us, and moods disquiet us. But the peace of Jesus that counteracts these is not a mood. It is more than that, more than contentment or a sense of comfort. The world also has the "peace" of quiet and of acceptance, insofar as it seeks earnestly for what is nobler. But it lacks the soul's consciousness of having found its inmost destiny and its true life in God. This consciousness is the firmly grounded certainty that the crucified Savior alone is the source and sustainer of our peace, because he has done away with sin, which allows no peace.
>
> Peace is constantly new and fresh, like a river that flows continually onward with new water and never stagnates or runs dry. It is the enduring experience of Christ in us, who wants to remain in us so that we remain in him.
>
> Moods and feelings come and go. They are incentives of the love that urges us to take hold of Christ's guiding hand. Gradually the character is strengthened from within, and in the end the fluctuations of the nervous system may be as oppressive as the worst weather, but upset the inner life just as little.
>
> When a strong wind blows against the current of a river, the surface is disturbed, and ripples arise; it is as if the water were being pulled upstream. Yet the current cannot change course. In the depth of the riverbed, it flows on no matter how strong the gales that blow against it. So let people do with us what they will. If peace reigns in our souls, we will be assured of our course, and nothing can shake us.

In my book *Be Not Afraid*, I address something that seems to pose the greatest challenge to human confidence: our universal fear of death. I will not elaborate on it here, except to say that even this threat to peace can be overcome through the assurance that comes from faith – and through love, which the apostle John says casts out fear.

If anyone had a reason to fear death, it was Martin Luther King, Jr. Immensely charismatic and unabashedly outspoken, he put his life on the line for the cause of racial equality time and again. In the end, as we know, he paid the ultimate price. Like anyone else, King must have been afraid of dying, yet the few times I met him or heard him speak, he radiated a deep calm and peace. Here was a man with no doubts as to his mission, and no crippling fears about the cost of carrying it out.

"No man is free if he fears death," he told the crowd at a civil rights rally in 1963. "But the minute you conquer the fear of death, at that moment you are free." Friends urged him to take fewer risks, but he shrugged them off. "I cannot worry about my safety," he told them. "I cannot live in fear. I have to function. If there is one fear I have conquered, it is the fear of death…I submit to you that if a man hasn't discovered something that he will die for, he isn't fit to live!"

Magdalena Boller, a member of my community who lost her mother to sudden death when she was a teen, experienced freedom from fear in very different circumstances. In remembering the experience, she touches on an important point: once peace fills the heart, it can be passed on to others.

> In my life, peace came in a strange and most wonderful way, overflowing from my mother in an hour of great need.
>
> My youngest brother Felix became critically ill when he was only nine months old, and died suddenly. We lived in an isolated region of South America, and the available medical

help was limited and primitive. At the time my mother wrote in her diary:

> Felix's pulse is very weak. Monika, our nurse, gives him a camphor injection, and I feel the pulse beating once more...Then suddenly his eyes open wide, and still wider, heavenly blue...But now, now these eyes are glazing over. I am the only one who notices it. "Moni, he is dying!" I cry out. We fold our hands. The words of our prayers go up to heaven in fervent pleading: "Lord, give him life, if it is thy will." O, I know better; the decision has already been made; he is released. "Jesus, come!" The words are wrung from our hearts. Yes, Jesus has come. He has come to take this child to himself. And yet the little heart still beats weakly. Another injection, and then artificial respiration, till at last we know it is too late.
>
> Give my child into my arms! Monika gives him to me. My baby lies on my lap and quietly, softly, his tiny soul goes into eternity. Or is it not as though eternity comes to us? At my side, dear Leo feels this too. There is such peace around us and in us. Calm, eternal calm. Our child returns to the angels from whom he came. Be silent. Do not speak now. My child, with what great pain I bore you. Is this joy or pain that fills my heart? I do not know. I know only that I give my child back to God, who gave him to me. And now: slowly, slowly my child grows cold upon my lap.

It was a Sunday morning. The rest of us children had just come back from a walk, and a neighbor took me aside to tell me that my little brother had died. I was devastated and ran wildly to his room. My mother was there. She looked at me with such love and tears, and put her arm around me: "Felix has gone to Jesus," she said. Her peace and acceptance overwhelmed me.

Nine years later my mother died suddenly, and her death was especially painful for me. I was just seventeen and had been away from home for almost a year, except for one or two weekend visits. Mama was the heart of our family, and she and I had been very close. Now she was gone, and I had missed the last year of her life. I simply could not accept the news of her death. How could this have happened?

In my despair, the image of my mother's tearstained but radiant face came back to me. I saw her standing there at my little brother's bedside those many years ago. And as I remembered the scene, the same reassuring peace she had shown me in her grief flowed into my heart, as if it were a parting gift from her.

The peace Magdalena felt may seem a rare thing, and in a sense it is. Yet Jesus promises the same to each of us. "My peace I give to you." Perhaps it is uncommon only because so few of us are willing to accept it. Tolstoy writes:

People question my lack of fear and suppose that there is something mystical in my view of life and death. But there is nothing of the kind. I like my garden, I like reading a book, I like caressing a child. By dying I lose all this, and therefore I do not wish to die, and I fear death.

It may be that my whole life consists of such temporary desires and their gratification. If so, I cannot help being afraid of what will end these desires. But the more I let these things give way, and replace them in my heart with another desire – the desire to do the will of God, and to give myself to him – the less I fear death, and the less does death exist for me. And if my desires be completely transformed, then nothing but life remains, and there is no death.

To replace what is earthly and temporary by what is eternal is the way of life, and along it we must travel. But in what state his own soul is – each one knows for himself.

Wholeness

How can we not lose our souls when everything and everybody pulls us in different directions? How can we "keep it together" when we are constantly being torn apart?

Jesus says, "Not a hair of your head will be lost. Your perseverance will win you your lives" (Luke 21:18–19). We can only survive our world when we trust that God knows us more intimately than we know ourselves. We can only keep it together when we believe that God holds us together. We can only win our lives when we remain faithful to the truth that every little part of us, yes, every hair, is completely safe in the divine embrace of our Lord. To say it differently: when we keep living a spiritual life, we have nothing to be afraid of.

Henri J. M. Nouwen

No matter how unique each person's search for peace may appear, a common thread ties them together. To a greater or lesser extent, everyone is on a journey toward wholeness. Some people say they are seeking peace of mind; others, peace of heart. Some are searching for fellowship, and others for community. Some are looking for inner serenity; others, global harmony. Underneath, all of these quests are motivated by a sense of the fragmentation of life, and by the desire for it to be overcome.

Charles Headland, a member of my church who died in his eighties, told me it was the compartmentalization of his life that set him searching for peace. As an accountant with a large firm, he had one set of friends; as a peace activist, another; as a church member, still another; and finally, his family. Nothing connected these sectors, and each day had to be balanced so as to fulfill his commitments to all four.

John Hinde, a fellow pastor, says he was also uncomfortable with his lifestyle when he became a pacifist shortly before World War II. As an active participant in the peace movement by night and on weekends, he did what he could to speak out against armed conflict. By day, however, he worked as an insurance broker at Lloyd's of London and felt he was contributing daily to the kind of class division and social conflict that creates war.

Life is full of divisions: between the home and the workplace; the private and the public; the job and the leisure-time activity; the political, the professional, and the personal. In itself, there is nothing wrong with that. The problems begin when these separate realms create contradictions and conflicts. Before long, inconsistency can become compromise, and after that, even hypocrisy. Barbara Greenyer, another church member, provides a telling example:

> In the late 1930s, in an attempt to promote communication and greater understanding, our church peace group had invited members of the Hitler Youth from a church in Germany to stay with us in our homes. Only one girl (I am still in touch with her) came. Soon after she returned home, war was declared, and I remember the shock of realizing that she was now our "enemy."
>
> To protest the killing, my husband, Kenneth, and I decided we would have nothing to do with the war effort. We refused to take gas masks or to build an Anderson shelter; we believed the Defense Department was trying to give the public a false sense of safety. Then Kenneth received a letter from one of

the senior stewards at our Wesleyan Methodist church, for-
bidding our peace group to meet on the premises, and telling
him what he would do to Kenneth if he were his son. It was an
angry letter. I wanted to go to this man and have it out with
him, but Kenneth reminded me that this man's son was out
fighting on the front line, and that we must have compassion.

We complied with the steward's letter, but then faced the
question of our relationship to the church. Could we take part
in Sunday meetings when they supported the war? We felt
we couldn't and wrote to the minister. He pleaded with us,
but we stood firm. It was a hard decision, because for both of
us the church had been the center of our lives. We had both
served there in the Sunday school…

Daniel Berrigan has written on the "fragmented conscience" that lies at the root of such a dilemma. In peacetime,
priests and ministers preach on the Ten Commandments,
"Thou shalt not kill…" In wartime, they bless bombers.
Anti-war people are pro-abortion, and militarists are anti-
abortion; anti-abortion activists are pro-death penalty, and
so on. "Everyone wants to get rid of some particular evil,
after which they feel the world is going to be a better place.
They forget that you can't be for the bomb and for children
at the same time…"

Rabbi Kenneth L. Cohen has said much the same. In one
essay he reminds readers of the horrifying two-facedness
of Nazi life, where friendly husbands and fathers, who
were also professional killers, "shot Jews in the morning
and listened to Mozart in the afternoon." The example is
extreme, but it highlights the potential end of every path
where conflicts run unresolved and threaten not only
peace, but life itself.

Christ's answers to this are simple, and devastatingly
clear: he says that the inside must become like the outside

(and the other way around); that everything must be lost, so it can be found again; that our lives must be given up, so they can be saved. He demands a seamless integrity that joins every aspect of life, a consistent battle in favor of all that is life-bringing and good, against everything that causes destruction and death.

Is wholeness a pre-condition for God's peace, then, or a result of it? Is it a "stepping stone," or a fruit? As a mark of the abundant life offered us by Christ I see it as a sign of peace – something that flows from it – rather than a pathway to it.

Charles Moore, a former seminary instructor who recently came to us with his wife, longed for wholeness in his life but could not find it. Eventually he concluded that as long as he was at the center of his personal search he would never find a satisfactory answer. Only if he allowed Christ to become the focal point of his life could everything find its true place.

> When I reflect on my life even ten years ago, I see that I was living a slow death of gradual disintegration. The explosive energy of my youth was fast becoming dissipated, not because of reckless living, but as a result of obsessively attempting to hold everything together. It was a meltdown of my own choosing. I was obsessed with trying hard, being good, meeting needs, pleasing God, and doing the right thing. There were so many good causes to join, so much knowledge to master, so many people to meet, so many relationships to build, so many obligations to fulfill, and so many opportunities to explore. But as I plunged into the whirlwind of possibility I became systematically fragmented. Peace of heart slipped away, peace of life was lost.
>
> How all this happened is easier for me to see now than it was then. My "self" was simply unable to integrate the

disparate, dangling threads of an over-committed existence. Individually and singly, the threads could not be joined together into a meaningful whole.

There was my work as a philosophy and theology professor, and my graduate studies. Both demanded my time; both demanded my allegiance. Joined together only in "idea," these two parts of my life were in fact worlds apart.

There were professional relationships with colleagues, too, who were "united" with me by our common faith, but who operated within entirely different structures and universes of discourse. Belief and practice were often at complete odds. I thought they could be bridged, and indeed, some attempts succeeded. But as life's demands increased, my strength did not. Besides, I was more than an academic self. I had other concerns, other interests. There was my personal life – my wife, Leslie, my friends and hers, my family and hers – with multifarious dimensions that never quite seemed to intersect. Sometimes they overlapped, but they never came together.

There was the church I attended and served at, but that was separate from the small intentional community Leslie and I were part of, and from the outreach ministry we were involved with in our depressed neighborhood. There were events organized by the activist groups I belonged to, functions at the institutions where I worked and studied, family gatherings I felt obliged to attend. I wanted everything, and I got what I wanted. But there was no existential coherence. I was fragmented inside and out.

Try as I did, I couldn't "get it together." Unable to let any one thing go, yet overwhelmed by keeping everything simultaneously under control, I created elaborate coping mechanisms which I perceived would get me through. I had a confidential counseling relationship with a close friend; I made opportunities for "release" through leisure, entertainment, etc., with my wife; I learned to reschedule my graduate studies and readjust my teaching load; I backed out of this or that time-consuming relationship, and so forth. But paring down, adjustment, and mending never did the trick. Well-intentioned and dedicated as I was, I was frantic and frayed, and my life remained disconnected.

It was also confusing. I thought that following Jesus meant expending oneself, being used up by God for his kingdom. Why, then, didn't I possess that promised peace, the peace that "passes understanding?" Why did I feel as if my life was being ripped apart? Why was I so frustrated, so on edge, so hassled? Our society is egotistical, individualistic, material-istic, and compulsive; it has little room for community. *My* needs, *my* desires, *my* strengths and weaknesses, *my* potential are the driving force; and my life is a fortress—fenced-off, guarded, and opened here and there to a select few.

Now that I look back, it seems ironic how full, yet how incomplete, my life felt. I had virtually everything I ever wanted: meaningful employment, intellectual excitement, altruistic outlets, caring friends, material success, and freedom to adjust my schedule whenever I felt the need to do so. But I was not at peace. The boundaries of my life were wide, and I kept all my options open.

In retrospect I see I was playing right into that grand deception: it's your life; do with it what you want. I had made my life the center of the universe, even under the guise of serving God. Despite my spiritual commitment and my efforts to live for God, I was trapped in the madness of a middle-class lifestyle that revolved—not only ultimately, but in the most mundane ways—around my wants and desires. I just couldn't see that this kind of living was unreal, untrue, unfit for the purpose for which God created us.

No matter how many ways I tried to compensate for the lack of synthesis in my life, it wasn't until I stopped living on terms set by the world (terms centered on personal ful-fillment and independence) that I began to find some sense of coherence. And I saw that I had a choice to make: I could continue living in that way, negotiating a multiplicity of demands and relationships of my own choosing; or I could begin anew on an altogether different foundation, one where community (not self), mutual service (not personal fulfillment), and God's kingdom (not mine) was the premise.

When Charles and Leslie heard about our community, they planned a visit, and a few years later they decided to come for good. Neither would claim that this is the calling for everyone, or even that "community" as such is the way to peace. But both say that the sense of wholeness they feel today is inseparable from the integration made possible by a life shared with others. "In community, the personal and the communal, the family-oriented and the work-related, the practical and the spiritual do not have to compete, but become as one. And all are nurtured and upheld by mutual commitment." Charles continues:

> I don't think the question of personal peace will ever go away entirely. I still struggle with the fact that who I am is far from what God intends me to be. Though the cross bridges this chasm, and I cling to it in faith, the battle of imperfection and sin still goes on. But the intent of my heart and the course of my actions are no longer at odds: the inner and outer dimensions of my life actually cohere; and they are held together, not strenuously, by force of will, but by a deep sense of God's peace.
>
> Today, having removed self from the center of my existence, I am more ready to surrender personal projects and goals, and to let go of life pursuits. God rules in my life in a new way. He has given me wholeness and a peace I never knew before.
>
> God created us for community, and for the generative, life-sustaining peace it brings. Community is no cure-all, but it offers a way of life where everything can come together as one whole. Divisions no longer exist. I am at peace with

myself, with others, and with God, and when I lose this peace I have a basis for fighting my way back to it (or being helped there by others). Instead of expending my energies on keeping my life together, I can forget myself and throw them into something much greater; something that pulls life together rather than ripping it apart.

My peace is far more than a personal blessing, for it is not really mine. It belongs to a greater whole, to a body whose members are not merely other people but brothers and sisters. It is the rich gift of God's peace. And the mystery of it is that it came into my life not because I struggled for it, but because my eyes were opened to see past the myth of self-fulfillment, and into the reality of a more abundant life. To experience this is to experience the grace of God. But it is also a choice.

Joy

There is nothing I can give you which you have not; but there is much I cannot give that you can take. No heaven can come to us unless our hearts find rest in today. Take heaven! No peace lies in the future which is not hidden in this present instant. Take peace! The gloom of the world is but a shadow; behind it, yet within reach, is joy. Take joy!

There is radiance and glory in the darkness, could we but see; and to see, we have only to look. I beseech you to look. Life is so generous a giver, but we, judging its gifts by their covering, cast them away as ugly, or heavy, or hard. Remove the covering, and you will find beneath it a living splendor, woven of love, by wisdom, with power. Welcome it, grasp it, and you touch the angel's hand that brings it to you.

Everything we call a trial, a sorrow, or a duty, believe me, that angel's hand is there; the gift is here, and the wonder of an overshadowing presence. Our joys too: be not content with them as joys. They, too, conceal diviner gifts.

And so, at this time, I greet you. Not quite as the world sends greetings, but with profound esteem and with the prayer that for you, now and forever, the day breaks, and the shadows flee away.   *Fra Giovanni*

In what has been called his most serious criticism of Christianity, Friedrich Nietzsche once complained that "the trouble with Christians is they have no joy." Yes, we know what happiness is; what makes us glad or pleased or even ecstatic. But joy? According to Molly Kelly, whose story I told earlier in this book, there is an important distinction.

> All of us have happy moments in our lives, but happiness is not joy. Joy comes only when you have peace. Happiness is often skin-deep, and fleeting; joy penetrates to our very soul; it is lasting. Happiness is a feel-good thing; joy can come with suffering. Happiness is often linked with winning; joy often comes with surrender.

Joy, then, is obviously the greater gift. Yet as Fra Giovanni says, it is often preceded by the disguised gifts of suffering or pain. Because we cannot accept these, and "cast them away as ugly, or heavy, or hard," we do not truly know joy.

Writing shortly before his death at the hands of his Nazi executioners, Ewald von Kleist implies that many Christians, even when they do accept suffering, cannot find joy because they hold such mistaken assumptions about its nature and meaning. He concludes:

> Every day it becomes clearer to me that we human beings (especially we of the white race, we Europeans) have put false valuations on everything, because we have become estranged from God. The world of today no longer has a true scale of values. People chase after fleeting goals and do not know what happiness is, nor where it lies; they no longer know what they should be thankful for.

Miriam Potts, a member of my church, says that for her, joy, gratitude, and peace are inextricably linked:

> If someone asks me, "Do you have peace in your heart? Are you at peace with God?" I hesitate. That is a question

I hardly dare to answer. How do I know? Sometimes I don't even know if I have faith.

But if someone asks me, "Do you have joy? Are you happy?" Then I can say an immediate, wholehearted yes! I love my work. I am happiest when I'm doing something for somebody else, like packing books for prison inmates. I am happiest when I'm busy, working till I drop into bed at night.

If I'm not happy, all I have to do is count my blessings, think of everything I can be thankful for, and then I'm happy again. But how can I be happy if I'm not at peace? Maybe it is the same thing...

For Ann (not her real name) the search for happiness and fulfillment went on year after year. Then she stopped looking out for herself and turned her life over to God.

When I think about peace, love, joy, and all the other things I have looked for in my life, I remember a question friends put to me when I first came to the community where I now live: why would a woman who has a loving husband, health, four beautiful children, financial security, and a home of her own want to give it all up to share her life with others?

To answer the question truthfully, I first need to explain that what they saw on the outside was a far cry from what they might have seen, had they been able to look inside my heart.

My husband and I were very active at church and among our friends in the congregation. We served others, shared with others, and felt a sense of happiness in being with others. Our gratefulness for fellowship, and our longing for more of it, led us to look for more community. We felt compelled to search for a greater commitment, and soon we were certain that Sunday Christianity wasn't enough. Nor was Wednesday-night bible study. For me, the big question was, "Is that all there is?" I had everything a woman could want, or at least I felt I was on the way to attaining it. Yet part of me was screaming inside: "I don't want 'everything.' There must be more to life than a nice spouse and children, a comfortable home, financial security." I grew desperate and scared. Why was I so unhappy?

I was raised in a home that looked pretty good on the outside. My mother and father worked hard, Dad as a factory worker and Mom as a housewife. We were a "strong" Catholic family who never missed Mass on Sunday, never ate meat on Friday, and went to confession once a month. In our parish things were strict: you did not want to fall into "mortal sin" and perish in hell. I learned to be afraid—afraid of making mistakes, afraid of being bad, afraid of God and what he might do to me.

People thought well of us, and no one knew the hell we were already perishing in. Dad was a decent, hard-working family man, and my mother loved us. As I look back on them now there are things I will always be thankful for. Many children go hungry and grow up without parents, it is true. Yet the fact is that many children in two-parent families with plenty of food suffer just as many atrocities. Their hurts are simply hidden—unspoken and invisible—behind a façade of normality, and no one knows what is really going on.

Nobody knew, for instance, that I was sexually abused by my older brother for three years, starting when I was six. Then he got a girlfriend. Nobody knew how my unstable teenage sister was beaten by my father with a belt in front of the whole family, simply because he could not cope with her and let his temper get the better of him. Nobody knew how a small thing such as spilling your milk at the dinner table was enough to put Dad into a rage that might last as long as two hours.

We lived in fear of making a mistake, of making Dad mad. After all, he drank a six-pack or more every night when he came home from work, and a case on the weekend. If he lost his temper after that, which happened several evenings a week, there was little any of us could do, including Mom, who sat there and bore it all silently. All evening long he would go on with his tirades, calling my mother one foul obscenity after another, and banging his fist on the table.

Later, at night, we would sometimes hear him start up again, yelling because my mother was not interested in "intimacy." We children would run for our rooms and put pillows over our heads, leave the house and go find a friend to hang out with, or turn up the volume on the TV. We were scared, bewildered, confused, and there was nothing to do but block out Dad's anger.

One thing I did to escape all the pain was sing. I used to sing and sing. I sang so much that my brothers and sisters would get very annoyed. "Well, at least I'm not fighting," I would say. I didn't realize it then, of course, but my songs were an outlet for my anxiety. I felt unloved and wanted so much to be loved. I thought: if I could be good and behave, others would be happy. If only there were peace in my family, I would be happy. When I was older I felt I couldn't do anything right, and that I wasn't worth much anyway. Things got worse in my teen years, and I got involved in all the usual perversities. The worst was that it was all hidden: the needs of my childhood, the sins of adolescence...

On the outside I was a "normal," "decent," even "religious" young woman. Yet on the inside there was turmoil and darkness. My life was one big lie. When I married, I half thought the problems might solve themselves, but they just carried on. Like my childhood and youth, my marriage looked fine from a distance, but to be honest, it was a mess.

When I was a little girl, I knew I needed God, and my despair would drive me to pray for help. Not that I expected him to help me. I didn't really think God loved me. I was bad, and I was convinced God wouldn't love someone like me. The more I wanted to be loved and cared for, the harder I grew, and the less capable of accepting love.

Now, as a married woman with a growing family, I still had no peace. I had known self-doubt and self-hatred for a long time, but now I began to project those feelings on everyone else. I hated the whole world. I was angry, and I felt rejected and worthless. I was an emotional wreck.

More than anything, I needed freedom from the pain of my past, but I looked for it in all the wrong places. To be honest, I was looking for one thing, and I went after it with a desperate passion: I wanted to be loved. I looked for love in my husband, Bob, and felt he failed me; I looked for it in my friends, and they also failed. I thought I looked for it in God, too. I went to a prayer center for Christians to receive counseling and to pray for healing. "Jesus loves you and forgives you," I was told. Somehow it remained outside my grasp. I could not feel his love or experience it. The counseling might have been beneficial to some degree, but it gave me no lasting peace of heart. Still I could not and would not give up.

Several years ago Bob and I decided to join this community. We felt God was calling us to full sharing with others, and answering that call brought us great joy and freedom. We sold our house, paid off some outstanding debts, and moved in. After about eighteen months, we asked to become full members.

During a sort of retreat in preparation for this, we tried to open our hearts to God and to brothers and sisters in the community, and to consider the course of our lives up to that point. It was a redemptive process, but very painful at the time, for it led us to the hard recognition that our marriage was a mess. We came to realize that we needed to face each other and God honestly, once and for all. We asked to leave the community; we felt we needed time and space both as a couple and as parents to reflect on what we really wanted in our deepest hearts. The community lovingly supported us in our decision, and helped us get established once more with a private house and work for Bob.

It was during this difficult period that I found peace – Jesus. But first I had to make the humiliating discovery that I was a completely self-centered person, hell-bent on my own happiness; and further, that I was full of hatred toward my husband, who I thought had failed me and who couldn't provide the love I so desperately needed and wanted. True, Bob had failed me in many ways, but I now saw that I was an emotional leech. For years I had been sapping what love he did have, and causing him to retreat. In short, the problem was me. Finally I could admit that my self-seeking was the main cause of my misery.

I asked God to show me the truth and help me, and this time I believed he would. He did. Suddenly I was able to feel remorse for the hurts I had caused others, instead of feeling sorry for myself and worrying about how others had hurt me. For the first time in my life, I even felt a desire to forgive those who had hurt me, especially my father. I felt remorse toward God, too, and in return I felt his love. I felt God's acceptance and forgiveness. In those days a passage from the Gospel of Mark came to my mind and became real to me – the one about how the healthy and strong do not need a doctor, but rather those who are sick. "I have not come to call the righteous, but sinners." What a relief flooded over me! I had been blind for years, and now, suddenly, I was beginning to see what happiness really was. The revelation of God's love to me as a sinner was overwhelming. It became the cornerstone for a new faith and gave me new joy in my heart.

As Bob and Ann began to talk things over, they saw each other as never before. They were able to forgive each other for everything that had made their marriage miserable, and move on. Soon they returned to our community and became full members. Ann goes on:

So how does life continue? Once you find peace, do you have it forever? I do not always have the feeling of peace. I have not always remained true to God's love. I still struggle with feelings of anxiety at times, or lapse into old worries and fears. I still have to fight to be genuine, to struggle against the temptation to please people or gain their approval. But when things overwhelm me, I have a battle cry: "Jesus is victorious in my body, my mind, my soul!"

I will always be a sinner. That's how I first came to God, not as a good person. But I don't need to waste energy thinking about it. There's enough to do, working for the kingdom. The more I put myself into that task, by serving others and forgetting about the old self, the happier I am.

There is fulfillment in doing things for others. It doesn't matter what it is. Some days I find happiness in baby sitting or cleaning; other days in preparing a meal for someone or doing their laundry. I am grateful whenever I get a chance to care for an elderly person.

I still have scars, I'm sure, but I am accepted as I am. In being able to give myself for others, I have received a gift I never found while seeking it for myself: pure joy.

Action

Time itself is neutral; it can be used either
destructively or constructively. More and more
I feel that the people of ill will have used time
much more effectively than have the people of
good will. We will have to repent in this generation not merely for the hateful words and
actions of the bad people, but for the appalling
silence of the good people. Human progress
never rolls in on wheels of inevitability; it comes
through the tireless efforts of men willing to be
coworkers with God, and without this hard
work, time itself becomes an ally of the forces
of stagnation.   *Martin Luther King, Jr.*

If anything is clear to the reader by this point, it should
be that peace does not mean inactivity. Peace can include
calm or repose. St. Augustine's oft-repeated quote – "My
heart does not find rest, until it rests in Thee" – contains a
deep truth. Yet what is "rest" in God? Is it complacence,
passivity?

The gift of peace is an answer to unfulfilled longing; it
is an end to the destructive wear-and-tear of doubt and sin.
It is wholeness and healing. But as much as it is all of these,
peace is also a call to action and new life. Peace may grow
out of prayer and meditation, but it cannot stop there. It
brings new obligations, new energy, and new creativity.
Like a seed beneath the soil, it germinates silently and
unseen, but then bursts with vitality, unfurling, flowering,
and finally coming to fruit.

In his book *Innerland* my grandfather writes that the end of time is not the end of activity: "The gates of the City on the Hill are not shut, but remain open." In the same sense, we who have received the gift of peace cannot keep it to ourselves, shutting out the noise around us and ignoring the plight of those who do not possess it:

> It is well and good to have achieved peace and quiet in this life, yet those who do are often tempted by the human tendency to ignore the basic will of Jesus: that once the heavy-laden soul is renewed, it must become a source of strength and energy for action. To sink spinelessly into a dumb stillness means being utterly useless for the life to which Jesus calls us.

Speaking from the perspective of engaged Buddhism, with its equal emphases on meditation and on compassionate commitment to others, Thich Nhat Hanh recalls the Vietnam War and the dilemma it posed for him. Was the fruit of peace contemplation, or was it action?

> So many of our villages were being bombed. Along with my monastic brothers and sisters, I had to decide what to do. Should we continue to practice in our monasteries, or should we leave the meditation halls in order to help the people who were suffering under the bombs? After careful reflection, we decided to do both—to go out and help people, but to do so in a spirit of engaged mindfulness...Once there is seeing, there must also be doing. Otherwise, what is the use of seeing?

If we seek to live in peace with our fellow human beings, certain inescapable responsibilities will fall on us, and we must grapple with them as Thich Nhat Hanh and his monks did. We cannot choose to live in harmony just with God, or just with ourselves, to the exclusion of others.

After my mother joined our community movement in her early twenties, she struggled for months to discern what peace meant in concrete terms. She wanted to devote herself to God, yet at the same time she was unsettled by a question her family and friends had put to her: how could she do anything for world peace if she wasn't "in the world" anymore?

In a letter to her mother, she admitted she had no fool-proof answers, yet felt certain that to live for peace, she must break away from the strife of bourgeois life and follow a different course. This did not necessarily mean a life of pious inactivity:

> Our community does not seek the peace of a hermit's life, or reject the world and its people just so we can pursue our own goals undisturbed. No! We take an active interest in current events, national and international, so that we may be led together to action and a clear stand…We are not afraid to express our convictions strongly and openly, and to put them into practice for all to see. That is what counts. It is not a matter of secluding ourselves within a set of monastery walls to go the way we have chosen in peace and quiet.

"Peace and quiet" were the very opposite of what my mother was looking for, and the same is true for many people who have turned against the meaninglessness of the middle-class rat race. When a person sets out to find peace, the search springs from the desire to find a deeper, more truly fulfilled life, not an emptier one. Veterans and businessmen, housewives and ministers, high school dropouts and educated professionals have all told me the same: peace does not just mean saying no to violence, greed, lust, or hypocrisy. It means saying yes to something that takes the place of all these.

In an earlier chapter I told of John Winter, a former lab employee who left his job after discovering that his firm was involved in ammunitions testing. He says:

I rejected violence and began to look for peace, but soon I realized that peace is much more than the absence of war. I was tired of saying I couldn't join the army. What could I do? I was seeking a practical alternative to war, not just an end to it. I wanted to commit myself to a different way. I wanted something to live for, not just something to fight against.

Gertrud Dalgas, a teacher who joined my grandparents and their little community in 1921, only months after its founding, felt the same. At that time she wrote in a magazine article:

> Our vision is of a kingdom of peace and nonviolence, a kingdom of freedom rooted in God. The critique and rejection of the prevailing conditions demand of us a positive counter-move, as an example. But precisely because we criticize capitalism, class hatred, murder, war, and deceit in social relationships, we feel compelled to dare a totally new and different life. We are merely a handful of people from various classes, trades, and professions. But we are not just refusing to bear arms or refuting the values of society at large in a negative way. We are building community against the demands of state, church, private property, and economic and social privilege.

Neither Gertrud, nor John, nor anyone else I have quoted would claim that the answer to the problems of the world is community in itself. But they would surely agree that if peace means action and commitment, it demands a fight. So would Dick Thomson, a Cornell graduate I have known for forty years. He writes:

> As a young man of twenty, I knew very well that peace was hardly to be found in the present world. I grew up during World War II, with the newspapers full of war news and propaganda, culminating in the dropping of the atomic bombs on Japan. I well remember the battles between John L. Lewis

and his mine-workers' union and big business management too. My mother voted Democrat, while my father voted Republican, but neither had much to say about God, and I found nothing attractive or hopeful in what I saw of religion.

If I had a god, it was science and the human mind, and I was encouraged to think I had an especially sharp one. Yet how little I knew of all the unpeace in the world, or even in myself, having never suffered war, poverty, oppression, serious illness, or any mental challenge I thought I could not meet. As I grew older, however, I was hounded by guilt over besetting sins I could not overcome, and by an inner discord that only became more intense, the more I tried to solve it.

Jesus says, "My peace I give unto you: not as the world giveth," and yet, "Think not that I am come to send peace upon the earth: I came not to send peace, but a sword."

At the community where I now live I met ordinary men and women who had discovered peace and joy in a united conviction that they had found the central fight of life. They knew what (or whom) they were fighting for. For the sake of their Lord, they were ready to face any suffering or need.

Here was a peace that struck my heart: not a withdrawing into death-like silence and passivity, but just the opposite: the peace of forgiveness and a new start in life, the peace of courage and activity and outspoken opposition to evil in all forms, along with love to all people.

When I asked about the source of this peace and joy, which I had never experienced in my life before, I was told, "Jesus Christ." Without seeing, I would not have believed, but this was real. It was then that I realized I had found the fight to which I, too, could and must give my own life.

I know that my experience is not unique to this community, and that God's kingdom is not limited to those who call themselves Christians. The idea of finding peace "in the fight" is there in the writings of early Quakers—George Fox, Isaac Pennington, and many others of their day who experienced the rebirth of faith amid the dead ashes of formal religiosity. It is also there among political prisoners and prisoners of conscience I have gotten to know. These men and women may speak a different language and live more radically than I do, but they are close in heart and spirit to what I've tried to describe, even if the press has unfairly demonized them as crazy radicals because of their unpopular positions on race and social justice. When you correspond or visit with them, you sense that despite the hardships they have suffered (some of them for many years) they have joy and peace. They are passionate, but not violent or irrational. And they know what their fight is: to reveal the truth as they recognize it, and to stand by it.

Again, when I came to this community as an unpeaceful young man, it was this same peace that moved me, a peace that radiated from people who knew what battle they were in, what war they were waging.

When God gives us his peace or love or joy, it remains his, and we cannot take it with us or keep it as our own. So long as it pleases him to give it to us, it is available. If we lose the gift, by slackening in the fight, or for any other reason, God still holds it in his hands and we can go back to him for it.

We cannot use the gift of peace: it uses us! To the extent that our own will takes over, we lose it. But this is our richness: we know where we can find it again.

Author Amy Carmichael uses the imagery of a battlefield to describe peace. She says that a soldier lying in bed while the battle is on does not have peace, but rather he who gives his life on the field. Those who fight closest to the captain are most likely to be wounded, but they will also have the greatest peace.

People talk about peace all the time; everybody wants it, no one is against it. But who is ready to commit himself to working for it to become a concrete reality? For each person, the call to action will take a unique form. For one it may lead to activism; for the next, to community; for the next, to an entirely different calling. It may simply mean being a voice of reconciliation at one's place of work, or trying to be more forgiving and loving at home.

A great deed may be nobler than an ordinary, unnoticed one, but it can distract us from the things we ought to be doing right around us. It can even produce a hardness of heart toward those who need us most. Jean Vanier warns, "Sometimes it is easier to hear the cries of the poor and oppressed who are far away than the cries of brothers and sisters in our own community. There is nothing very splendid in responding to the person who is with us day after day and who gets on our nerves."

Wherever we are and whatever we do, there will be sacrifices to make and commitments to fulfill if our peace is to bear fruit. For unlike the false peace that mixes everything and commits one to nothing, God's peace comes as a bracing wind and sets into motion everything that stands in its path.

> If we go no further than individually edifying encounters with Jesus, we are missing the greatness of his cause. That is why we are told to seek the kingdom of God and its righteousness first: so that we might become worthy not only in the sense of personal blessedness, but as fighters for his kingdom.
>
> Let us live more intensely in the expectation of the Lord! If we do not wait for him in every aspect of our life, we do not wait at all. I ask myself every day: have I hoped enough, fought enough, loved enough? Our expectation of the kingdom must lead to deeds. *J. Heinrich Arnold*

Justice

The motive is love of brother, and we are commanded to love our brothers. If religion has so neglected the needs of the poor and of the great mass of workers, and permitted them to live in the most horrible destitution while comforting them with the solace of a promise of a life after death when all tears shall be wiped away, then that religion is suspect. Who would believe such Job's comforters? On the other hand, if those professing religion shared the life of the poor and worked to better their lot, and risked their lives as revolutionists do, and trade union organizers have done in the past, then there is a ring of truth about the promises of the glory to come. The cross is followed by the resurrection.

Dorothy Day

Of all the slogans I have heard at demonstrations and rallies over the last decades, one of the simplest and strongest is "No justice, no peace." If it is important to talk or write about peace, then praying for it and working for it in some practical way is even more important. But when all is said and done, peace is real only insofar as it gives birth to justice.

In the Letter of James we read, "What good is it, my brothers and sisters, if you say you have faith, but do not have works? Can faith save you? If a brother or sister is naked and lacks daily food and you say to them, 'Go in peace, keep warm, and eat your fill' and yet do not supply their bodily needs, what is the good of that?" And Christoph Blumhardt writes, "In the final analysis, our whole spiritual life is of no significance if it does not show tangible, visible earthly consequences."

In the same way as the injustices of social inequality, oppression, slavery, and war go hand in hand with strife and division, so peace must go hand in hand with justice, for justice flourishes where these things are overcome. Given the state of our planet today, it is not surprising that people dismiss both peace and justice as utopian foolishness. How can anyone be at peace, they ask, when turmoil and anguish are everywhere, and stockpiled weapons of mass destruction mock the very idea of human survival? How can there be justice, when the whims of a shrinking handful of wealthy and powerful men wreak havoc with the lives of millions around the globe? In 1934, speaking on the connection between private property and war, my grandfather said, "There is no justice whatever. Stupidity reigns." What would he say today?

Some people may insist that the spirit of peace is alive and well, even if hidden under the cloak of hypocrisy here and there. I am not so sure. Unless the justice and peace we preach is grounded in deeds, it is no more than an empty phrase. We remain pious frauds, like those of whom Jeremiah complains, "They dress the wound of my people as though it were not serious. 'Peace, peace,' they say; yet there is no peace."

On the other hand, even if we fail over and over in staying faithful to the vision of God's kingdom, and in seeking to live according to its spirit, it does not change the fact that God is still a God of peace. His reign is one of justice, truth, and love. If our faith is a sham, that is not his fault, but an indictment on us. "What a pity, that so hard on the heels of Christ come the Christians." (Annie Dillard)

The peace of the kingdom calls for a new social order and a new relationship among people. That is why Jesus urges us to stand with the poor and oppressed, with the prisoners and the sick. It is why he says, "Blessed are the peace*makers*." It is also why he commands us to "go out into all the world" and proclaim his peace as the good news. If anyone rejects this peace, he says, we should shake the dust from our feet and move on. Therefore we need to be led to all those who long for it.

In December 1997 I traveled to Chiapas, Mexico, to meet with Bishop Samuel Ruiz García. Don Samuel, as he is known, has been nominated for the Nobel Peace Prize on account of his work with the people there, especially the indigenous peasants who populate the region's impoverished mountain villages.

Don Samuel is dedicated, very simply, to what he calls the twofold task of peace and justice. That task has included mediating between the government and the Zapatistas, a grassroots movement organized to fight for basic human rights such as land ownership and access to medical care. Not surprisingly, his outspokenness has earned him hatred and harassment, especially from the repressive local government, and he has been the target of at least two assassination attempts. During our conversation, Don Samuel told me:

> Peace for humanity is not only the absence of war, or the end of violence. The Romans said, "If you want peace, prepare to fight." For them peacetime was the time to prepare for war. It is for us, too, but in a different way. For us Christians, peace is based on a fundamental new relationship between mankind and God. That is why Christ said he brought peace, "not as the world gives." He brought a different peace.

Within today's society, that peace has to be conceived and built on the basis of justice: the kingdom of God, which is a kingdom of peace, a kingdom of justice, truth, and love. That is why for us peace has deep social foundations and deep spiritual foundations. That is why peace demands a new social order. It demands a new brotherly relationship among people. And it requires a change in the oppressive socio-economic structure.

We understand that peace is a gift from God. Christ said, "I give it to you. I give you my peace." But peace is also a task; it is work that we have to develop. In that sense, the presence of the poor man in relation to the kingdom is a sacramental presence of Christ. Christ is present through the sacrament of the poor man, because he himself said that the final and only question we will be asked is that of our love for Christ. "I was hungry, and you gave me something to eat. I was thirsty, and you gave me something to drink." When did we do this? "When you did it to these my brothers, you did it to me." It is not a question of doctrine, but of practice. I will not be asked whether I made mistakes, but I will be asked whether or not I loved my brother.

Peace comes from the poor man. He is at the center of the way to peace. The poor man defines the history of human society. A man is poor as a result of a social conflict. There is a system that makes him poor, a system that deprives him. If in a society the poorest person is the reference point for the common good, then we have a society that is doing its task. But if in a society the poor man is squashed on the floor, that society is opposed to the kingdom.

Often we turn a deaf ear to people like Don Samuel. Prejudice and fear lead us to shut out their voices, to dismiss them, or even to silence them by killing them.

Admittedly there are individuals among those who embrace the cause of justice who are not peacemakers in the Christian sense of the word. Some are decidedly unpeaceful, and a few even advocate armed revolution. Yet even where we differ as to goals and means, we must acknowledge that they are the voices of the oppressed, and that there can never be true justice and peace on earth unless there is also justice and peace for them. Their fight may take place in a different trench, but it is a fight for the same freedoms and rights we white Europeans and Americans take for granted – at the cost of their lives. So long as we ignore this fact, we have no right to denounce their struggle.

In the early church, Christians fed the hungry at their own cost; they clothed and sheltered the naked and homeless at a personal sacrifice. It would have been unthinkable for them to talk about peace without talking about justice. And their contemporaries said about them, "See how they love each other." Nowadays things are quite different. As Catholic Worker cofounder Peter Maurin writes:

> Today the poor are no longer fed, clothed, and sheltered at a personal sacrifice, but at the expense of the taxpayers. And because of this, the pagans say about the Christians, "See how they pass the buck."

Christoph Blumhardt noticed the same lack of care among the pious believers of his generation, and never wearied of railing against it. He saw the root of the problem as a selfish preoccupation with salvation, coupled with a complete disregard for one's fellow human beings:

> There are parties in Christendom who are already rejoicing that they will be transfigured and float up to heaven. But that is not the way it will be. It is time to take up a task in which we are the first to be judged, not the first to receive a sofa in heaven. For only those who are truly first – first to stand before the Savior in judgment – can become tools to further his righteousness.

Frankly, I think many good Christians will be surprised to see who is there when the angels gather the "elect" from the corners of the earth. The older I get and the more deeply I see the enormity of injustice in our society, the more convinced I am that if Jesus really came for those "who hunger and thirst for justice and righteousness," then his chosen ones must include the homeless, the prisoners, the outcast, and the forgotten – the wretched of the earth.

We are quick to forget it, but Jesus' values stand in direct opposition to ours. His justice turns human justice on its head. He said that the first shall be last, and the last first; that he who loses his life shall save it, and he who tries to save it will lose it.

What does it mean to lose one's life? For Jesus it meant abandoning every privilege and every defense, and taking the lowliest path.

> Before Jesus died, he said he would be delivered into the hands of those in authority: the pious, and the state. He would have to surrender, defenseless, to their power. And when his disciples asked, "Couldn't we invoke the powers at our disposal? We could call fire down from heaven, and lightning from the clouds," Jesus asked them, "Do you not know which spirit you belong to?" You have forgotten the Spirit! You have forgotten your highest calling. You leave the Spirit the moment you take up the cause of force instead of love, even if you call upon heavenly fire and heavenly lightning and heavenly miracles. *Eberhard Arnold*

For us who claim to be followers of Christ, the use of violence or force cannot even be considered as a means to achieve justice. Yet that does not give us the right to buttonhole others, to coax or persuade them to agree with our way of thinking. We cannot address the struggling third-world peasant, the urban anarchist, the policeman, or the soldier, and say, "Lay down your weapons and go the way of love and peace."

Faith is not given to everybody, nor is it everyone's concern at every moment. Even if it were, it might not be apparent in a way that we could understand. In my experience, the answers to life's most important questions do not arrive in neat packages. Sometimes they do not come to us at all; it is we who must go after them, by trial and error, and with long struggle.

In her book *On Pilgrimage*, Dorothy Day reflects on the thorny issue of how the Christian must balance the demands of justice with those of peace. She provides no simplistic solutions but reveals a good basis for any search: humility.

> It is a sure thing that the freedom God endowed us with is a terrible gift, and he has left us to do the job of plowing through the morass of sin and hatred and cruelty and the contempt that is all around us. It is a morass that we ourselves have made.

> I can sympathize with the instinct of righteous wrath that leads people to take to arms in a revolution, when I see the forgotten aged in mental hospitals, and men sleeping in doorways on the Bowery or fishing in garbage cans for food; and families in the slums, often with no heat in such weather as we have been having, and migrants in their shanty towns...

> We are certainly not Marxist socialists, nor do we believe in violent revolution. Yet we do believe that it is better to revolt, to fight, as Castro did with his handful of men, than to do nothing...Until we ourselves as followers of Christ abjure the use of war as a means of achieving justice and truth, we are going to get nowhere in criticizing men who are using war to change the social order.

Speaking at the height of the Civil Rights Movement, Martin Luther King Jr. addressed the same issue – the criticism of those who stand on the sidelines, talking about justice but continually disparaging any attempts to do something toward it. "Over the past few years I have been gravely disappointed with the white moderate…who is more devoted to 'law and order' than to justice; who prefers a negative peace, which is the absence of tension, to a positive peace, which is the presence of justice."

Others, especially many young northern African Americans, felt King was far too cautious and ineffectual, and disdained his belief in the power of Gandhian nonviolence. King refused to espouse their less peaceful methods of working for change, but neither did he condemn their tactics outright: "If the oppressed are denied the right to carry out revolution peacefully, how can they be condemned when they turn to violent revolution?"

In Psalm 85 we read, "Justice and peace shall kiss; truth shall rise up, and righteousness smile down from heaven." If we have faith in this promise – if we believe that these words can become reality, not only in some glorious hereafter, but on this earth – then we must be willing to risk everything. We must reject injustice in every form, whether economic exploitation, social inequality, racial division, or political oppression. Yet we must also reject all violence, from military service and armed revolution to police brutality and the abuse of women and children.

For us the justice of God's kingdom is based on something very different from the balancing of interests or rights. It is far more radical than the humanist conceptions of liberty, equality and fraternity; more basic than the opportunity to compete. It is a justice born of love, and it is rooted in our willingness to die for each other.

Unless we are actually ready to do this, to lay down life itself for the sake of our brothers, all our talk about peace is meaningless.

Certainly we do not and cannot live in a sinless state. But the way some people speak about the necessity of evil and about our common bondage in guilt often leads to a lazy consent to the status quo. How can we presume to dismiss the world peace to which the prophets witness, the elimination of government proclaimed in John's Revelation, the overcoming of the present social order by brotherhood and community? How can we avoid the great either-or that Jesus has put before us: God or mammon? Too many of us have turned away from the clarity of Jesus; too many of us have weakly accepted man's paradoxical situation in relation to God; we say yes and no, no and yes at the same time to everything. Where is our urge to fight?

People may exclaim, "Surely you don't want to wage a general campaign against all evil!" But that is exactly what it is all about. For this Jesus came to the world, and he has called us and sent us out so that we might take up and carry on this fight. He came to destroy the works of the devil. He is perfect light, and in him there is no darkness. *Eberhard Arnold*

Hope

Wherever God is, his peace draws near. His presence brings freedom from inner restlessness, dividedness, and hostile impulses; it brings harmony of heart, mind, and soul. But he is a living God, and therefore he is action just as much as he is peace. And on the foundation of the harmony he bestows, he brings into being a broader unity. This unity is the joy of love; it is oneness of purpose and action, community, brotherhood, and justice for all.

Eberhard Arnold

Peace is a life-giving power. It heals what is broken, replenishes what is used up, and unleashes what is knotted and bound up. Peace brings hope where there is despair, harmony where there is discord, love where there is hatred. It brings wholeness where there is fragmentation, consistency where there is compromise and deceit. Peace penetrates every sphere of existence, the spiritual as well as the material, the material as well as the spiritual. If it does not accomplish this transformation, it is not true peace at all, but sheer fancy.

Peace comes from God, but its reach encompasses the earth. And when its power holds sway, it transforms people and structures. It is cosmic in aim, but it begins quietly, sometimes imperceptibly, from within. Where peace rules, there is unity of self with true self, man with woman, God with man. There is unity between vine and branch; temples are cleansed; bodies are healed.

None of this can happen by itself, or in a vacuum. Throughout this book we have seen that the way of peace has nothing to do with passivity or resignation. Peace is not for the spineless or self-absorbed, or for those content with a quiet life. Peace demands that we live honestly before God, before others, and in the light of our own conscience. It does not come without the burden of duty, for it demands deeds of love.

Peace is a relentless pursuit kept up only by hope and courage, vision and commitment. Thus the search for it cannot be a selfish one. It cannot be merely a question of achieving closure, finding fulfillment or, as Aristotle put it, actualizing our human potential. No! To seek peace means to seek harmony within ourselves, with others, and with God. It means working for the unity Christ envisioned in his last prayer: "May they all be one, as thou, Father, art in me, and I in thee; may they also be one in us, so that the world may believe that thou hast sent me."

Even when we are at peace with God and feel at one with him, the difference between our human pettiness and his greatness as our Creator ought to devastate us. But we cannot let this recognition defeat us. Kierkegaard writes: "We need to put away our fears and stop living a life shielded against responsibility before the truth... We must enter into a fullness of life where everything we do is done in relation to the eternal."

Grandiose as this sounds, it is really very simple. When our eyes are on the eternal, we will be motivated by love – love for our neighbor, spouse, enemy, and friend – and we will seek to live in harmony with all people and all living things. "For if you do not love your brother, whom you can see, how can you love God, whom you cannot see?" If we do not have peace, it is probably because we have forgotten to love one another. And there is no excuse for that. I do not believe that anyone is so lacking in gifts that he cannot love. Thérèse of Lisieux writes:

> Love gave me the key to my vocation. I realized that if the church was a body made up of different members, she would not be without the greatest and most essential of them all. I realized that love includes all vocations, that love is all things, and that, because it is eternal, it embraces every time and place.
>
> Swept by an ecstatic joy, I cried, "At last I have found my vocation. My vocation is love! I have found my place. *I will be love.* So I shall be everything and so my dreams will be fulfilled!" Why do I speak of ecstatic joy? It's the wrong phrase to use. Instead, I should speak of peace, that calm, tranquil peace that the helmsman feels as he sees the beacon that guides him into harbor. How brightly this beacon of love burns! And I know how to reach it and how to make its flames my own.

Most of us do not have half Saint Thérèse's enthusiasm. On the contrary, as Christoph Blumhardt notes, peace and unity are missing from our lives:

> We are stuck fast in a web of gossip and lies, hatred, envy, full of poison… We fight and envy each other even in the name of Christ. It seems to go on forever, with one man taking offense at the next, and no one able to make peace. We are so far from being a people who truly carry the gospel in our hearts and follow the Savior in a practical way!

Yet he goes on, "But why should our hearts not open wide and become free, so we can be brothers and sisters? Why should we not have hope?"

Rabbi Hugo Gryn, a survivor of the Holocaust, learned the importance of hope as a young boy in Auschwitz, where he was imprisoned in the same barracks as his father:

Despite the unspeakable conditions, many Jews, including my father, held on to whatever observances they could. One midwinter evening an inmate reminded him that it was soon the first night of Chanukah, the feast of lights. Over the next days my father constructed a small menorah of metal scraps. For a wick, he took threads from his prison uniform. Instead of oil, he somehow managed to wheedle butter from a guard.

Such observances were strictly verboten, but we were used to taking risks. What I protested was the "waste" of precious calories. Would it not be better to share the butter on a crust of bread than to burn it?

"Hugo," said my father, "both you and I know that a person can live a very long time without food. But I tell you, a person cannot live a single day without hope. This oil will kindle a flame of hope. Never let hope die out. Not here; not anywhere. Remember this."

Rabbi Gryn's story touches on a truth discovered by many before and after him: ultimately, it is hope that makes it possible for us to live from day to day.

The apocalyptic vision gives us the hope that, despite considerable evidence to the contrary, in the end it is good that will prevail. In John's Revelation we find justice restored and a God who comes to be with those who have suffered the most in a cruel, unjust, and violent world. A God who does not roar and strut like the ultimate dictator, but who gently "wipes away all tears from their eyes."   *Kathleen Norris*

If we have faith, there ought to be nothing that keeps us from acting on that hope now. We may "wait patiently for the Lord," as the Gospel instructs us, but if we are truly expectant, there will always be action in our waiting.

On the last day of 1997, in Chiapas, Mexico, hundreds of Tzotzil Indians walked in a memorial procession to the village of Acteal, where forty-five of their compatriots—mostly women and children—had been brutally killed by a local pro-government militia just nine days before. Living in an isolated area where political repression has resulted in one "disappearance" after another, the participants knew they were not marching without danger.

Unarmed, the marchers were doubly vulnerable because of their position: though supportive of the goals of local Zapatista freedom-fighters, they remained opposed to the use of force and were thus accused by both sides of partisanship and disloyalty. Yet the procession was not just a gamble. It was an act of defiance undertaken in a spirit of determination and hope.

A sign on a wooden cross at the head of the crowd read, "It is time to harvest, time to build," and many of the men carried bricks ("to symbolize the weight of our suffering," one said) which they planned to use to build a shrine for the dead. Several planned to resettle in the village, though they knew they might have to flee again. And carrying a cracked statue of the Virgin Mary "in the name of peace," they remained committed to nonviolence.

Who were these courageous men and women who could stare death so calmly in the face? Was their peace the mark of some strange martyr-like strength? A sign of insanity? Maybe they simply felt like Phil Berrigan's wife Elizabeth McAlister, who wrote after her husband's latest imprisonment:

> God's vision—more, God's promise—of a humane and just society is a promise on which we can bet our lives. None of us can be content until this promise is a reality for all people and for all our earth. So you stake your life on the vision of God in Isaiah, the days to come when people will beat swords into plowshares and spears into pruning hooks; so we endure and

are carried by our God in that endurance. Putting flesh on God's vision today, you are part of bringing it into being – no more, no less.

In a passage in *The Brothers Karamazov*, Fyodor Dostoevsky writes with similar hope and faith. The conversation is between Father Zossima (when he is still a young man) and a mysterious stranger:

"Heaven," the stranger said, "lies hidden within all of us – here it lies hidden in me now, and if I will it, it will be revealed to me tomorrow and for all time."

I looked at him. He was speaking with great emotion and gazing mysteriously at me, as if he were questioning me.

"And that we are all responsible to all for all, apart from our own sins, you were quite right in thinking that, and it is wonderful how you could comprehend it in all its significance at once. And in very truth, so soon as men understand that, the kingdom of heaven will be for them not a dream, but a living reality."

"And when," I cried out to him bitterly, "when will that come to pass? And will it ever come to pass? Is not it simply a dream of ours?"

"What then, you don't believe it," he said. "You preach it and don't believe it yourself? Believe me, this dream, as you call it, will come to pass without doubt; it will come, but not now, for every process has its law. It's a spiritual, psychological process. To transform the world, to recreate it afresh, men must turn into another path psychologically. Until you have become really, in actual fact, a brother to everyone, brotherhood will not come to pass. No sort of scientific teaching, no kind of common interest, will ever teach people to share property and privileges with equal consideration for all. Everyone will think his share too small, and they will always be envying, complaining, and attacking one another. You ask when it will come to pass. It will come to pass, but first we have to go through the period of isolation."

"What do you mean by isolation?" I asked him.

"Why, the isolation that prevails everywhere, above all in our age – it has not fully developed, it has not reached its limit yet. For everyone strives to keep his individuality as apart as possible. Everyone wishes to secure the greatest possible fullness of life for himself and forgets that true security is to be found in social solidarity rather than in isolated individual efforts. But this terrible individualism must inevitably have an end, and suddenly all will understand how unnaturally they are separated from one another. It will be the spirit of the time, and people will marvel that they have sat so long in darkness without seeing the light. And then the sign of the Son of Man will be seen in the heavens.

"But until then, we must keep the banner flying. Sometimes, even if he has to do it alone, and his conduct seems to be crazy, a man must set an example, and so draw people's souls out of their solitude, and spur them to some act of brotherly love, that the great idea may not die."

Index of Names

The Author

Johann Christoph Arnold's books on children, marriage, death, peacemaking, and forgiving have sold over 400,000 copies in English and have been translated into numerous languages. A writer with an uncommon wealth of experiences and personal insights, he has counseled thousands of individuals over the last forty years, including married couples, children, and teens; addicts, prison inmates, and law enforcement officers; educators, students, and the terminally ill.

Arnold is a senior pastor of the Bruderhof, an international community movement based on Christ's teachings and the practices of the earliest Christians, who shared all things in common. Arnold has traveled extensively on behalf of the movement and met with religious leaders around the world, including Martin Luther King, Jr., Pope John Paul II, Mother Teresa, and Desmond Tutu.

Arnold is a frequent guest on talk shows and a popular speaker at schools and conferences internationally on forgiveness and nonviolent conflict resolution. He has participated in initiatives for peace, justice, and reconciliation around the world. Recent journeys have taken him to Europe, the Middle East, Central America, Southeast Asia, and Africa – and into schools, hospitals, prisons, and refugee camps.

Arnold and his wife, Verena, have eight children and over forty grandchildren, and live in upstate New York.

Other Titles by the Author

Why Forgive?

No matter the weight of our bitterness, forgiving is the surest way to get out from under it. In this book survivors of crime, betrayal, abuse, bigotry, and war share their amazing stories to challenge and encourage others wherever they are on the road to healing.

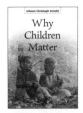

Be Not Afraid

In this hope-filled book, ordinary men and women offer hard-won insights on dealing with uncertainty, loss, grief, and the fear of death. Through their real-life stories, Arnold shows how suffering can be given meaning, and despair overcome.

Why Children Matter

Raising a child has never been more challenging. Arnold offers time-tested wisdom and common-sense advice on what children need most, what holds a family together, and how to rediscover the joy of parenting.

Sex, God & Marriage

A refreshing new look at sex, love, and marriage that sees past the usual issues and gets to the root: our relationship with God, and the defining power of that bond over all other relationships.

Plough Publishing House
151 Bowne Drive
PO Box 398
Walden NY 12586
www.plough.com.